BODIED, AND WELL
MEN,
LINATION TO JOIN THE TROOPS,

NGTON,
THE
PENDENCE
TATES,
enemies,

# OTICE,

# YANKEE DOODLE DAYS

### Exploring the
### American Revolution

*For Dick*
*Enjoy our history*

*Lincoln Diamant*

CHRISTMAS 1996 at FARMINGTON
FROM MOLLY

Other Books by Lincoln Diamant:

*Chaining the Hudson: The Fight for the River*
*Bernard Romans: Forgotten Patriot of the American Revolution*
*Stamping Our History* (with Charles Davidson)
*Aristotle: An Introduction*
*The Anatomy of a Commercial*
*Television's Classic Commercials*
*The Broadcast Communications Dictionary* (Editor)

# YANKEE DOODLE DAYS

## Exploring the
## American Revolution

### LINCOLN DIAMANT

PURPLE MOUNTAIN PRESS

Fleischmanns, New York

Portions of Chapters IV, IX, and XII have appeared in different form in *Military Affairs, Columbia Today*, and the *Hudson Valley Regional Review*.

*Yankee Doodle Days: Exploring the American Revolution*

FIRST EDITION
1996

Published by
PURPLE MOUNTAIN PRESS, LTD.
Main Street, P.O. Box E3
Fleischmanns, New York 12430-0378
914-254-4062
914-254-4476 (fax)

**Library of Congress Cataloging-in-Publication Data**

Diamant, Lincoln.
    Yankee Doodle days : exploring the American Revolution / Lincoln Diamant. - - 1st ed.
        p.    cm.
    Includes bibliographical references and index.
    ISBN 0-935796-73-8 (cloth : alk. paper)
    1. United States- -History- -Revolution, 1775-1783- -Anecdotes.
    2. United States- -History- -Revolution, 1775-1783- -Biography--Anecdotes.    I. Title.
    E296.D53    1996
    973.3- -dc20                                                    96-17054
                                                                        CIP

Manufactured in the United States of America
Printed on acid-free paper
1  3  5  7  9  8  6  4  2

FOR JOAN, ROLF, NORA, and TONY

With special appreciation to
Rolf Diamant, Harold W. Lustig, Nora Mitchell,
Lloyd Moss, Charles A. Nelson, Vyvyan Pinches,
Michael Pope, Nicholas W. Puner, Susan Ray,
Hugh Van Dusen, and Richard C. Wiles.

# CONTENTS

# Preface

*"Waiving all considerations of right and wrong, I ask---is it common sense to use force toward the Americans? Not 20,000 troops, not treble that number, fighting 3,000 miles away from home and supplies, could hope to conquer a nation fighting for liberty."*
> ---JOHN WESLEY, WRITING TO LORD DARTMOUTH,
> SECRETARY FOR THE COLONIES, 14 JUNE 1775.

*"If I were an American as I am an Englishman, while a foreign troop is landed in my country, I would never lay down my arms. Never! Never! Never!"*
> ---WILLIAM PITT, EARL OF CHATHAM, IN THE
> HOUSE OF LORDS, 20 NOVEMBER 1777

*IN 1984*, the Library of Congress issued *Revolutionary America*, a remarkable two-volume, 1,672-page descriptive bibliography listing more than 15,000 popular and scholarly books, pamphlets, and magazine articles exploring every aspect of the American War of Independence. Some of the materials cited are old, some new, some rare, some remaindered; but each riffle in this flood is marked by its author's irrepressible urge to set down some new aspect of what the poet and scholar Robert Graves has called "the most important single event of modern times."

Two centuries after this political and military upheaval changed the lives of two and a half million British North Americans, it still grabs the imagination. The sheer size of today's Revolutionary War bookshelf prompts an author's nervous fear that his widow's mite of research or interpretation may be the last straw that sends everything crashing to the floor. I hope this will not be the case with this book.

*Yankee Doodle Days* is not an exercise in historic deconstruction. Rather, it is a companion down some less traveled but parallel pathways of our rebellious past. Because I believe that history, like politics, begins at home, all but one of the Revolutionary trails traced in this volume lead through the State of New York and the County of Westchester, where I have made my home for half a century. This is not intended to diminish in any way the valiant efforts of revolutionists of the Southern and Middle States; their equally dramatic stories are merely left to other writers.

In this book, the reader meets a varied group of American patriots, each marching to a slightly different rendition of "Yankee Doodle." They are men and women whose stories over the years have captured my interest and deepened my understanding of the people who made the American Revolution. There are no illustrations to accompany the text; most of my subjects were neither wealthy nor eminent enough to be of interest to a limner of their time. As for illustrations of inanimate objects, a cannon still looks like a cannon; a musket like a musket.

*BEGINNING WITH* George III[1], many of the world's leaders have found it expedient to deny the significance of America's eight-year struggle for independence—and how this profound military and political realignment turned the new "united states" of former British North Americans into a wild card among the world's existing power structures. As recently as 1988, then Soviet President Mikhail S. Gorbachev insisted before the United Nations that there were only two revolutions in world history worthy of the name. The American Revolution was not one of them.[2]

---

[1] Despite the oft-repeated assertion of the Crown's continued economic dependence on the Colonies, none of George III's ministers—nor ministers of any prior sovereign—ever bothered to pay a visit to British North America.

[2] "Two great revolutions," proclaimed the eventually deposed Soviet president, "the French Revolution of 1789 and the Russian Revolution of 1917, exerted a powerful impact on the very nature of history and radically altered the course of world events."

No one in the General Assembly, not even the United States delegate, requested the floor to redress the startling omission. Yet it was our comparatively bloodless upheaval that paved the way for the other two political turnarounds, each with its particular and far more sanguine challenges to the divine authority of kings and tsars.

Our Revolution and the Constitution it engendered laid the foundation for a unique polyglot nation of a culturally diverse group of inhabitants living side by side in varying degrees of harmony and disharmony. As we fretfully slide towards a new millenium, we can still celebrate the continuity of this country that Thomas Jefferson, in his First Inaugural address, proudly hailed as "the world's best hope."

*Pondside*
*Ossining, New York*
*July 4, 1995*

# CHAPTER I

# Marching Song

*IN WHICH a few anonymous Continental Army poets and musicians turn a derisive British jape into America's first—and jauntiest— song of defiance.*

*THOSE FAMILIAR WITH* French history can tell you the story of Claude Joseph Rouget de Lisle, who, in 1792, wrote the words and music for the "Marseillaise." His spirited battle hymn celebrated the expulsion of royalist troops from the Paris Tuileries by revolutionary volunteers from Marseilles.[1]

Compared to the unambiguous origins of what was to become the French national anthem, those of America's first battle hymn are shrouded in mystery. The exact year in which Americans first sang "Yankee Doodle" is not known, but there certainly were local variations on the verses among the colonials a decade before the Revolution.

Until musicologists dug into the problem a quarter century ago, most Americans cherished a myth about this national air: they believed that the catchy, high-stepping tune that became the Continental Army's marching song was created by a talented British army doctor, Richard Schuckberg.

In 1754, during the French and Indian Wars—so ran the story— Shuckberg was stationed at colonial "Fort" Crailo, an old Dutch farm building on the Crailo property near Albany, New York. Reportedly, he was seated on the edge of a well, watching with

---

[1] Curiously, De Lisle himself was a royalist soldier, stationed far from Paris. At one point, he came close to being guillotined by the revolutionaries.

amusement as a Regular Army sergeant attempted to drill a hapless handful of ill-dressed New England recruits. The recruits' inept responses to their sergeant's "hay foot, straw foot" commands inspired the good doctor to whip out his pencil—like Francis Scott Key at Baltimore half a century later—and set down some stanzas and a chorus mocking the young colonial militiamen. Shuckberg could not have anticipated, the story concludes, that twenty-one years later some anonymous Continental Army poets, in a burst of musically irreverent snook-cocking, would revolutionize the original song, preserving only the chorus and transforming the other verses into the new nation's first and greatest patriotic hit.

There is another theory, however, that claims that "Yankee Doodle" was not dreamed up by Dr. Shuckberg at all, but by another British song-and-dance man, Edward Bangs, two decades later to while away the tedium of the long American siege of Boston.

In any case, "Yankee Doodle" was first published in 1775. No matter who was responsible for the song, it remains a sprightly part of the American cultural heritage. Every child learns at least the first verse and chorus at its mother's knee:

> *Yankee Doodle went to town,*
> Riding on a pony.
> He stuck a feather in his hat,
> And called it macaroni.
>
> Yankee Doodle, keep it up,
> Yankee Doodle dandy,
> Mind the music and the step,
> And with the girls, be handy.

As Americans began their long military struggle for political independence, a new set of verses—199 of them—replaced those of the more comedic and even salacious original song, which soon disappeared. The new material included a series of vignettes reflecting the milling excitement of Continental Army camp life from the point of view of a naive and astonished patriotic youngster. The new song's colorful and egalitarian stanzas went on and on, making "Yankee Doodle" one of the longest marching songs on record. Here is only a taste:

*Father and I went down to Camp*
Along with Captain Good'n,
And there we see the men and boys
As thick as hasty puddin'.

Other verses reflected basic Yankee values, including thrift:

*And there we see a thousand men*
As rich as Squire David,
And what they wast'd every day,
I wish it could be sav-ed.

The [mo]lasses they eat every day
Would keep a house a winter,
They have as much, as I'll be bound,
To eat when they've a mind-ter.

There were descriptions of various artillery pieces:

*And there we see a swampin' gun*
Big as a log of maple,
Upon a deuc'd little cart—
A load for Father's cattle.

And every time they shoot it off,
It takes a horn of powder.
It makes a noise like Father's gun—
Only a nation louder.

Cousin Simon grew so bold
I thought he would have cock't it.
It scairt me so, I shrink't it off
And hung by Father's pocket.

The bayonets and bombs were fearsome:

*And Captain Davis had a gun*
He kind of clap't his hand on't,
And stuck a crooked stabbin' iron

Upon the little end of't.

And there I see a pumpkin shell
As big as Mother's basin,
And every time they touch'd it off
They scamper'd like tarnation.

I see a little barrel, too,
The heads were made of leather,
They knock't on it with little clubs
To call the folks together.

The lyrical New England levelers even aimed jabs at the Virginia
planter they had accepted to command their siege at Boston:

*And there was Gen'ral Washington*
All gentlefolk about 'im,
They say he's grown so 'tarnal proud
He will not go without 'em.

He had him on his meetin' clothes,
And rode a strappin' stallion,
He set the men along in rows—
In hundreds, and in millions.

The flamin' ribbons in his hat,
They looked so tearin' fine, ah,
I wanted pockily to get
To give to my Jemima.

"Yankee Doodle" even jokes about the "necessaries"—the privy
pits—intended to service the vastly overcrowded camp:

*I see another snarl of men*—
A-diggin' graves, they told me—
So 'tarnal long and 'tarnal deep,
They 'tended they should hold me.

It scairt me so, I hook't it off

Nor stop't, as I remember—
Nor turn'd about till I got home,
Lock't up in Mother's chamber.

There is no guarantee that these words are exactly those sung by the marching revolutionists, since no one at the time bothered to transcribe them; but the tradition for them is strong.

It once was assumed that Dr. Shuckberg's satiric talent also extended to early musical jingle writing, but musicologists tell us the tune of "Yankee Doodle" has been claimed at one time or another by France, Spain, Germany, the Netherlands, and even Hungary. In the end, it turns out to be a traditional accompaniment for the old English nursery rhyme, "Lucy Locket lost her pocket, Kitty Fisher found it, etc.," whose tune, in turn, evolved from an earlier game song, "Fisher's Jig." Many composers across a classical-to-popular spectrum—from Henri Vieuxtemps, Anton Dvorak, Charles Ives, Daniel Gregory Mason, and William Mayer, to George M. Cohan—have incorporated the notes of "Yankee Doodle" into their compositions.

Without delving too deeply into etymology, it should be noted that H. L. Mencken traced the "mysterious origin" of the term "Yankee" to 1683, "at which time [it] denoted a Dutch West Indian pirate. By the middle of the 18th century, it had come to mean any New Englander." "Doodle" is derived from the German word for "simpleton." As to the feather, this probably refers to Oliver Cromwell once derisively adding a feather to his military hat. "Macaronists," Ellen Moers tells us in her scholarly book *The Dandy*, "were that circle of affected, oddly-dressed, cosmopolitan Londoners who can be identified as the nearest ancestors of the Regency dandies." Yankee Doodle's feather thus may have mocked the elaborate, effeminate, powdered, and pommaded hairdos and wigs of a mid-18th-century group of London fops, frequently the butt of military and cartoonists' ridicule.

BEFORE LONG, both Americans and British were using the popular song as an instrument of political propaganda. New lyrics were crafted at the drop of a feathered hat. One such verse, set down in 1778 by Revolutionary poet Francis Hopkinson in his rollicking

"Battle of the Kegs," unabashedly explained the military inactivity of the enemy commander in chief, Lord Howe:

*Sir William he, snug as a flea,*
Lay all this time a-snoring;
Nor dreamed of harm, as he lay warm
In bed with Mrs. Loring.[2]

When the Catholic Louis XVI entered the war on the side of the rigorously Protestant Americans, the British made comment in verse:

*The French Alliance then peep'd forth,*
The papists flocked in shoals, sir:
Friseurs, marquis, valets of birth,
And priests to save our souls, sir!

The impromptu lyrics became increasingly ribald, and the music played on and on. Military custom gave a defeated army the choice of one of the victor's marching songs to play mockingly at the surrender ceremonies. Accordingly, Burgoyne's bands serenaded the Americans at Saratoga with "Yankee Doodle."

One of Burgoyne's officers ruefully observed: " 'Yankey-doodle' is now their paean, a favorite of favorites, played in their army, esteemed as warlike as the 'Grenadier's March.' It is the lover's spell, the nurse's lullaby. After our rapid successes, we held the Yankees in great contempt, but it was not a little mortifying to hear them play this tune."

When Cornwallis angered Lafayette at Yorktown by first attempting to surrender his army to the French command, rather than to the Americans, the Marquis prevented the British bands from playing "Yankee Doodle," and they were forced to fall back on "The World Turned Upside Down." Otherwise "Yankee Doodle" could have been said both to have begun and ended the Revolution.

---

[2] Elizabeth Loring was the complaisant blue-eyed blonde wife of the former Boston tory British Commissary of Prisoners Joshua Loring, Jr.

*THE CONTINENTALS* did not require a full military band to play their anthem; they found it equally inspiring—perhaps more so—tootled (doodled?) on a fife or two, with a lad on the drum. It is obviously this tune that is being played in Archibald Willard's grand old Centennial painting, "The Spirit of '76."

At one point, Washington feared the infectious tune might turn the American reoccupation of Philadelphia into too much of a troop frolic. On 23 August 1777, he ordered "all drums and fifes to be collected at the center of each brigade, and only the 'Quick Step' to be played, with such moderation that the men may step to it with ease—without dancing along, as too often has been their wont."

Ten years later, with the Revolution finally won and the country now throbbing with argument over the wisdom of supplanting its unwieldy Articles of Confederation with a new federal Constitution, "Yankee Doodle" was again pressed into service to play down dissension and play up a budding nationalism:

Now politicians of all kinds
Who are not yet decided;
May see how Yankees speak their minds
And yet are not divided.

"Yankee Doodle" has continued to serve in all American wars since the Revolution; it even sounded in the streets of far-off Tucson, Arizona, on 20 May 1862, when the town was liberated by Union troops from a Confederate force under General Henry Sibley.

*GREAT BRITAIN* never really forgave America its expropriation of "Yankee Doodle." More than sixty years after the Revolution, *Punch*, the British satirical magazine, commented on the Oregon boundary dispute by picturing a corpulent John Bull holding at arm's length an unkempt, cigar-chawing, slave whip-carrying, pugnacious dandiprat labeled "America." In the caption, England asks, "What? You young Yankee-Noodle, strike your own father!"

Yankee Doodle, keep it up.

# CHAPTER II

# General Washington's Indians

*IN WHICH the Commander in chief experiences difficulty with the idea of recruiting Native Americans, and misspeaks to Congress.*

*IN MAY 1775,* even before George Washington impressed the rebellious Second Continental Congress in Philadelphia by wearing his Virginia militia uniform, a handful of Native American—"Indian"—volunteers were fighting (and dying) around Boston for the colonists' Revolution. By 15 June, when his fellow delegates apppointed Washington supreme commander of the Continental Army, the American forces at Cambridge, Massachusetts, included at least seventeen Native American Minutemen from Stockbridge.[1]

All had been recruited from that western Massachusetts settlement by the Bay Colony's Provincial Congress for service in the Revolution's earliest military actions. Except for the color of their skin, these Native American soldiers resembled the other young New Englanders bivouacked around Cambridge. They had long forsworn traditional deerskin breechclouts, fringed jackets, and leggings. They wore colonial shirts and trousers. They had permanently abandoned

---

[1] In 1734, the (Scottish) Society for Propagating Christian Knowledge had established a mission at Stockbridge, a surviving "fire place" of the Muhheakunnuk (Mohican) nation, near the Massachusetts-New York border. The missionaries' aim was to teach the native population the use of European agricultural implements, like axes, plows, and hoes, "changing their whole habit of thinking and acting, raising them into the condition of a civil, industrious and polished people, instilled with principles of virtue and piety." Acculturation of the Christianized natives came quickly.

bent sapling-and-bark "long house" construction in favor of log cabins, frame meeting houses, and a substantial church.

By the end of the 1760s, the Stockbridge Indian population also included many of the surviving Muhheakunnuk People. This "Wappinger" nation had an immediate interest in the success of the American rebellion. For more than a decade, the Wappinger sachems' attempts to utilize the British legal system to recover more than 200,000 stolen acres[2] had met with failure.

While away fighting for the British in the French and Indian Wars, the Wappinger men had lodged their women, children, and old men at Stockbridge, intending for all to return to their land after the fighting was done. But the Philipse Family, an immensely wealthy and powerful New York colonial clan, took the fighting men's absence as an opportunity to appropriate the land, using expired patents, illegal grants, and forged deeds. Upon the warriors' return, all attempts to recover their land proved futile. The sachems' 1767 trip to England to plead their case before George III's ministers only produced empty promises.

Sir William Johnson, the King's Northern Department Superintendent of Indian Affairs and ostensible protector of Native American interests, wrote candidly on 26 August 1765 to Roger Morris, a Philipse heir: "I have laid it down as an invariable rule, from which I never did nor ever shall deviate, that where a Title is set up by any Tribe of Indians of little consequence or importance to His Majesty's interests, and who may be considered as long domesticated, that such claim had better remain unsupported than that Several old Titles of His Majesty's Subjects should thereby become disturbed."[3]

---

[2] Present-day Putnam County, New York, with a population of 84,000 in six towns and three villages.

[3] But mindful of chief Wappinger sachem Daniel Nimham's recent audience with the Queen, Sir William—under whose command Nimham had loyally served against the French—cagily hedged his bets: "On the contrary, wherever a just complaint exists, made either by the natives themselves, or by Connections who I knew would resent neglect, I judge it my duty to support the same—even though it should disturb the property of any man. An Indian claim may be very just, although pronounced otherwise by law. A Patent obtained in a most iniquitous manner cannot be supported whilst any virtue and sound policy remain among us."

*WHAT WASHINGTON* thought of the celebrated Wappinger vs. Philipse lawsuit is not recorded. Although it dragged through the New York Colony courts for more than a decade, it was a "northern" legal matter and Washington was a Virginian. Still, as a young visitor to the City, he had enjoyed Philipse hospitality and even danced with the future Mrs. Roger Morris, heiress to a fortune far exceeding that eventually secured by Washington in his marriage to Daniel Parke Custis's widow.[4]

*THE WAPPINGER* legal actions to repossess their land coincided with a decade of repressive British colonial taxation. Each year leading up to Lexington and Concord gave birth to new economic and political contradictions. The Native Americans at Stockbridge watched hopefully as rebellious indignation rose among the colonial whites. Everywhere, military preparation increased, and the British blockade of Boston finally ignited open warfare. Simplistically, the Wappinger nation hoped that a change in colonial New York government would permit the reopening of their suit to recover their ancestral hunting grounds.

A major concern of every colonial legislature was maintaining adequate forces on the battlefield. Troop levies to the Continental Army were short-term and sporadic. Local militia support was enthusiastic but undependable. During the early days of the Revolution, Washington seemed more like a busy chief of staff than a field commander as he made his fervent appeals to Congress and the colonies for additional troops. When it came to considering Native Americans as possible recruits for the Continental Army, he seemed to be of different opinions at different hours.

This was the relatively untested Washington, reserved and conservative. He had not yet had opportunity to demonstrate his unique qualities of leadership, his practical judgment and poise (so exasperating to a later handful of personal enemies) in recasting the usual forms of 18th century warfare or in the preservation of a withering

---

[4] Washington would once again enjoy Mary Philipse Morris's hospitality, but in absentia. In September 1776, the American army used Roger Morris's handsome abandoned northern Manhattan mansion—in what would become Washington Heights—as a command post during a month of unfortunate military reverses around New York City.

army. The commander in chief's superb ability to prepare and wait—apparently to delay—until the proper military and psychological moment, would eventually win for him the profound esteem and universal confidence of his countrymen. But all that was still to come.

Whether Washington was pleased to see them there or not, Native American volunteers from Stockbridge, drawn from among the more than 200 natives enlisted as "Berkshire Minute Men" under Town Selectman Jehoiakin Mtohoxin, continued to serve with the earliest New Englanders in arms around Boston. From Concord, two weeks before Paul Revere's ride, the Massachusetts Bay Provincial Congress acknowledged their early participation in the common struggle:

> WHEREAS: a number of Indians, natives of the town of Stockbridge, have enlisted as Minute Men, for their encouragement, the sum of £23 be employed to purchase one blanket and one yard of ribbon for each, and the following address be presented to them: "It affords us great pleasure and satisfaction to hear that you, our Brothers, the natives of Stockbridge, have taken up the hatchet in the cause of liberty. We find you have not been inattentive to the unhappy controversy we are engaged in with our Mother Country: our rights and privileges have been invaded and our property taken from us without our consent. This is a common cause, a cause you are equally engaged in with ourselves; we are all brothers. If the Parliament of Great Britain takes from us our property and our lands without our consent, they will do the same by you; your property, your lands will be insecure. In short, not any of us shall have anything we can call our own. We have directed that each of you enlisted in the service have a blanket and a ribbon as a testimony of our affection.

The Massachusetts legislature forwarded the above resolution to the Stockbridge natives, who deliberated in tribal council for only two days and then authorized Sachem Solomon Uhhaunauwaunmut to ignore any ironies and make this graphic, generous, and judiciously partisan reply on 11 April to President John Hancock and the Provincial Congress:

> Brothers: We have heard you speak by your letter. We thank you for it; we now make answer. Brothers: You remember when you

first came over the great waters, I was great and you were little—very small. I then took you in for a friend, and kept you under my arms so that no one might injure you. Since that time we have ever been true friends; there never has been any quarrel between us. But now our conditions are changed. You are become great and tall; you reach up to the clouds; you are seen all around the world. And I am become small, very little; I am not so high as your heel. Now you take care of me, and I look to you for protection. Brothers: I am sorry to hear of this great quarrel between you and Old England. It appears that blood must soon be shed to end this quarrel. We never until this day understood the foundation of this quarrel between you and the Country you came from. Brothers: Whenever I see your blood running, you will soon find me about you to avenge my brothers' blood. Although I am low and small, I will grip hold of your enemys' heel, that he cannot run so fast and light as if he had nothing at his heels. Brothers: You know I am not so wise as you are, therefore I ask your advice in what I am now going to say. I am thinking, before you come to action, to take a run to the westward, and feel the minds of my Indian brothers, the Six Nations,[5] and know how they stand; whether they are on your side, or for your enemies. If I find they are against you I will try to turn their minds. I think they will listen to me, for they have always looked this way for advice concerning all important news that comes from the rising of the sun. If they hearken to me, you will not be afraid of any danger behind you. However their minds are affected, you shall soon know by me. Now I think I can do you more service in this way than by marching off immediately to Boston, to stay there (it may be) a great while, before blood runs. Now as I said, you are wiser than I; I leave this for your consideration, whether I come down immediately, or wait till I hear some blood is spilled. Brothers: I

[5] This highly organized political and military "Iroquois Confederacy" of Mohawks, Oneidas, Onondagas, Cayugas and Senecas in west central New York (excepting the Mohawks, a present-day county is named for each) adopted an additional sixth nation in 1722, the Tuscaroras (800 of whose Iroquoian-speaking members had previously been sold into colonial slavery in North Carolina). During the Revolution, all but the Oneidas eventually sided with the British. A decade after the Revolution, an Iroquois sachem ruefully observed, "Remember: When our father, the King of England, and the Americans quarreled, the Americans desired us red people to sit still, as we had no business in their dispute. But our Father put the hatchet into our hands to strike the Americans, and both Him and us were unsuccessful. From that moment our lands were torn to pieces, and the Americans triumphed as the greatest people in this great Island."

would not have you think by this that we are falling back from our engagements. We are ready to do anything for your relief, and shall be guided by your counsel. Brothers: One thing I ask of you, if you send for me to fight; that you will let me fight in my own Indian way. I am not used to fight English fashion; therefore you must not expect I can train like your men. Only point out to me where your enemies keep, and that is all I shall want to know.

In the gathering military storm, such positive Native American response was both a practical and a psychological support. It helped allay qualms held by many Massachusetts legislators about enlisting and arming "domestic Indians." Anticipating the positive reply from the Stockbridges, Congressional delegate John Hancock had also written the "Eastern Indians"—the St. John's, Nova Scotia, and Penobscot nations of the northeastern coast:

> Our good brothers, the Indians at Stockbridge, all join with us, and some of their men have enlisted as soldiers. We have given each one a blanket and a ribbon, and they will be paid in the service. If any of you are willing to enlist, we will do the same for you.

Three nights later, Paul Revere hung his lanterns in the belfry of Old North Church. The eruption of hostilities at Lexington and Concord threw all communications throughout the colony into confusion. It took more than a month for Sachem Uhhaunauwaunmut's response to reach the Provincial Congress, evacuated to Watertown, Massachusetts. On 8 June, the legislature directed Secretary Samuel Freeman to respond:

> To the Moheakounuck Tribe of Indians living in and about Stockbridge:
> Brothers: We this day, by the delegate from Stockbridge, first heard your friendly answer to our speech to you. We now reply.
> Brothers: You say that you once were great but are now little, and that we once were little and are now great. The Supreme Spirit orders these things. Whether we are little or great, let us keep the path of friendship clear which our fathers made, and in which we have both travelled to this time. The friends of the wicked counsellors of our King fell upon us and shed some blood, soon after we spoke to you last by our letter. But we, with a small twig, killed so many and frightened them so much that they have shut them-

selves up in our great town called Boston, which they have made strong. We have now made our hatchets and all our instruments of war sharp and bright. All the chief counsellors who live on this side of the great water are now sitting in the Grand Council-House in Philadelphia.[6]

When they give the word, we shall all, as one man, fall on and drive our enemies out of their strong fort, and follow them until they shall take their hands out of our pouches, and let us sit in our Council-House as we used to do, and as our fathers did in old times.

Brothers: Though you are small, yet you are wise. Use your wisdom to help us. If you think it best, go and smoke your pipe with your Indian brothers towards the setting of the sun, and tell them all you hear and all you see, and let us know what their wise men say. If some of your young men have a mind to see what we are doing here, let them come down and tarry among our warriors. We will provide for them while they are here. Brothers! When you have any trouble, come and tell it to us and we will help you.

Without delay, the Stockbridge natives kept their promise and sent messengers to the Six Nations. British agents promptly arrested the couriers as military spies, shipped them north to Montreal for court martial, and sentenced them to be hanged. The sentence created turmoil among the Native American populations. A number of leading sachems offered themselves as substitutes for the messengers on the Canadian scaffolds. A Stockbridge resident, writing to Hancock in Philadelphia, related how those chiefs had angrily told the British: "You offered us money to fight for you, but we would not take it, as we would have nothing to do with your quarrel. But now we shall know who are our enemies."

The British soon relented and freed the prisoners, but the lesson was not lost on native America. Before the Battle of Bunker Hill on 17 June, more than 30 young men from Stockbridge were already serving under Colonel William Goodrich (and later, Colonel John Paterson) on the Continental lines outside Boston. The names of 17 (phonetically rendered—Jehoiakim Naunuptauk, etc.) are preserved on an unusual petition concerning the availability of liquor.

[6] The Second Continental Congress, which convened May 10th and elected John Hancock its president.

Dated four days after the battle of Bunker Hill and addressed to the President of the Provincial Congress in Watertown, the petition read as follows:

> We whose names are hereunto subscribed, being soldiers enlisted in the Provincial Army during the summer, beg leave to lay this request before you. We in our more serious hours reflect with shame upon our aptness to drink spiritous liquors to excess when we are under temptation; by which foolish conduct when we are guilty of rendering ourselves unfit for usefulness and service to our fellow-men, and are also disagreeable to those that have anything to do with us. We are sensible that we injure ourselves more than anyone else. When we get a taste, we must with shame say, that sometimes no interest of our own will prevent us from procuring more, till we get too much. We therefore desire that you would in your wisdom do something during our residence here, that we may get so much as will be good for us, and no more. We further desire you to order the Paymaster-General to pay all our wages that are now or may be due to us when we are dismissed, to Timothy Edwards[7] or Jahiel Woodbridge, Esquires, Delegates from the Town of Stockbridge, and to them only or to their order, that they may be enabled to provide for us while we are here, what we may necessarily want; and bring all the rest home all together, and divide it among us as we like.

A committee appointed by the Provincial Congress duly approved the natives' petition, as follows:

> It is recommended and enjoined that all persons who sell spiritous liquors be particularly careful not to let the Stockbridge Indians enlisted in the American Army have too much strong drink, as that wholly unfits them for service.

TWO WEEKS later, after an eleven-day journey on horseback from Philadelphia, George Washington arrived in Cambridge to take command of the Continental Army. Then Native American recruitment and participation in the War of Independence entered a new phase.

The frustrating Revolutionary siege of Boston dragged on for eleven months. Although Washington strove to hold his little force

---

[7] Son of the distinguished nonconforming New England divine.

together, when most of the New England enlistments expired in the
fall of 1775, he allowed the Stockbridge natives to be dismissed to
their homes 150 miles away with no further encouragement, under
the new "native neutrality" policy of the United Colonies.

Early in January 1776, with distressing news spreading southward from the faltering Revolutionary invasion of Canada, the
commander in chief wrote respectfully to the influential head of his
Northern Army in Albany, New York, Major General Philip
Schuyler, concerning a half-dozen native sachems who had come to
visit the American lines at Cambridge. The chiefs were members of
the Caghnawaga nation living on both sides of the Canadian border.
Their allegiance—punctuated by the Deerfield Raid in 1704—had
whipsawed back and forth between the French and British during a
century of colonial warfare.[8]

The Caghnawaga sachems—all professed Catholics—had told
Washington they were ready to denounce their nation's current
neutrality and begin fighting for the American cause. Whereupon the
commander in chief candidly confessed to Schuyler:

> I am a little embarassed to know in what manner to conduct myself
> in respect to the Indians now here. They have—notwithstanding
> the Treaty of Neutrality which I find they entered into with you
> the other day (agreeably to what appears to be the sense of the
> Congress)—signified a desire to me to take up arms in behalf of the
> United Colonies. My embarrassment does not proceed so much
> from the impropriety of encouraging these people to depart from
> their neutrality, as from the expense which probably may follow.
> Their proffered services ought not to be rejected, but how far I
> ought to go is the question that puzzles me.

General Schuyler answered at once: "If we can decently get rid
of their offer, I would prefer it to employing them. The expense we
are at in the Indian department is now amazing."

But Washington had already made his decision without waiting
for Schuyler's reply. On 10 January, he advised President Hancock
in Philadelphia: "I shall write General Schuyler regarding the tender

---

[8] In 1990, descendents of the same nation held off Canadian police and military forces
attempting to convert part of their ancestral reservation into a surburban Montreal
golf course.

made by the Indians; not to call for their assistance unless he shall at any time want it."

Two days later, the commander in chief so notified Schuyler, mentioning that he had also seen fit to approve that General's earlier Treaty of Neutrality with the Caghnawagas, in which they had, according to Schuyler ". . .expressed much satisfaction, and said they were now happy and free, like the New England people."

BY SPRING, thousands of colonial conscripts and volunteers were flocking towards Boston. On the other hand, the "happy and free" Stockbridge Native American soldiers, among the first to answer the country's call, had also been among the first to be discharged home by Washington. Like so many other Continentals to come, their military service had been completely unrewarded. After a frustrating wait of almost four months, they petitioned the Province's Clothing Committee: "Be pleased to pay John Sergeant[9] our blanket and coat money entitled to us for serving as soldiers in the Army at Cambridge last summer."

Their written request, with thirty-two signatures, was certified from Charlestown, Massachusetts, on 12 March by Colonel Paterson:

"The within-named persons were soldiers in my regiment, and served as such until dismissed by His Excellency General Washington."

By April, the British had been checkmated out of Boston by heavy artillery seized at and sledded down from Fort Ticonderoga. The enemy set sail for Nova Scotia to regroup, while Washington faced the critical problem of obtaining additional troops for the Continental Army. Unexpected reverses and an outbreak of smallpox were afflicting the Revolutionary invasion of Canada. The next site of war would surely be New York. Preparing all available forces for the stoutest possible defense of that city, the commander in chief wrote to Hancock:

In my opinion, it will be impossible to keep the Indians in a state of neutrality. They must, and no doubt soon will, take an active part either for or against us. I would submit it to the consideration of the Congress, whether it would not be best immediately to engage them on our side?

[9] Son of the original white missionary to the Stockbridge community.

That same day, 19 April, the first anniversary of Lexington and Concord, Washington wrote in similar vein from New York to General Schuyler: "You who know the temper and disposition of the savages will, I doubt not, think with me that it will be impossible to keep them in a state of neutrality." He added, with slight exaggeration: "I have urged on Congress the necessity of engaging them on our side."

At the end of the following month, Congress summoned Washington to Philadelphia to discuss a burgeoning host of military problems, including Native American recruitment. Another delegation of Canadian tribesmen had just arrived in the City of Brotherly Love, importuning Congress for permission to enlist in the army. From Amboy en route to Philadelphia, the commander in chief wrote to Schuyler on 22 May: "Our situation respecting the Indians is delicate and embarrassing. I hope Congress's Committee will conduct the matter in a way that shall most advance the public good."

One of the suggestions Washington expected to place before the legislators in Philadelphia was simple: rather than put native troops on the Continental Army payroll, they should be allowed to serve as irregulars, with a piecework bounty paid for each British soldier they captured.

On 3 June, Congress finally bit the musketball. They empowered their commander in chief formally to employ up to 2,000 Native Americans—nations' army locations unspecified—on behalf of the American invasion of Canada. In North America, the dispossessors were finally appealing to the dispossessed.

Four days later, Washington wrote to Schuyler in Albany:

> I enclose a copy of a Resolve of Congress for employing and engaging a number of Indians in the service. Congress have not particularized the mode for raising and engaging them, so I would have you and the Commissioners for Indian Affairs[10] do what may seem best for securing their service. If a smaller number than 2,000 would do, I would not advise more to be embodied than may be necessary.

---

[10] Besides Schuyler himself, these commissioners for the Northern Military Department included Major Joseph Hawley, Turbot Francis, Oliver Wolcott, and Volkert Douw.

A skeptical reply from Schuyler awaited the commander in chief upon his return to New York City: "So far as being able to procure 2,000 Indians to join us, I shall be extremely happy if we can prevent them from acting against us." Nonetheless, Schuyler, plagued by old ailments that kept him hobbling between his bed and his saddle, went to work trying to locate 2,000 Native American volunteers.

Meanwhile, Washington grappled with a semantic problem. His Northern Army was now in full retreat from Canada, ready to recross the New York border, and he wrote for clarification from President Hancock:

> The resolve of June 3rd for taking Indians into service, if literally pursued, confines them to service in Canada. Was that the meaning of Congress? Or may the Commander in chief order their service in any place he thinks necessary?

Less than two weeks before the first Royal Navy warships and troop transports appeared in New York Harbor, a deeply concerned Washington, digging a flurry of entrenchments against the imminent enemy attack, dashed off this fateful note to Schuyler, containing a suggestion of Congressional approval:

> Knowing their [Congress's] sentiments fully upon this head, I cannot but advise that you forthwith hold a Conference with the Six Nations...and any others you with your Brother Commissioners may think necessary...without waiting further directions. The situation of our affairs will not suffer further delay.

Spurred by fears of disaster awaiting his sick, starving, exhausted, and dispirited Canadian expeditionary troops, Schuyler was hardly "suffering further delay." Even before Washington's dispatch rider thundered up the Hudson, Schuyler and the Commissioners for Indian Affairs, casting about for Native American inductees, set upon the most obvious source—Stockbridge.

As military pressures mounted, Washington again urged Schuyler on 16 June: "The sooner a Conference can be held the better."

The following day, Congress sat in Philadelphia as a committee of the whole. Presumably thinking of its "2,000 Canadian Indians," they authorized a bounty of $30 for every British soldier ($100 for an officer) captured by Native American allies.

Receiving word of the resolution, Washington immediately wrote Schuyler from New York City: "I am hopeful the bounty Congress have agreed to allow will prove a powerful inducement to engage the Indians in our service. You are authorized to promise them punctual payment." He also confirmed to Hancock in Philadelphia: "I have transmitted to General Schuyler your Resolves about the Indians, and requested his strict attention and exertions in order to carry them into execution with all possible dispatch."

But when Washington's original messenger came galloping back from Albany, it appeared that doughty General Schuyler had moved with far more dispatch and consequence than either his superior or Congress had intended. To a rump session of only himself and Commissioner Douw on 13 June (while Congress was still debating the bounty to be paid for captured Britishers), Schuyler had summoned Timothy Edwards, guardian of the Mohican Wappingers at Stockbridge, and. . .

> . . .laid before the Commissioners [all two of them] the Resolve of the Continental Congress transmitted by Your Excellency, 'that the General be empowered to employ in Canada a number of Indians not exceeding two thousand.' After having duly considered the same, the Commissioners came to the following Resolutions: That two companies, to consist of one captain, two lieutenants, three sergeants, three corporals and 175 privates be raised out of the Mohikander Indians with all possible expedition, to march without further orders.

These were to be the first interracial units in the American army. Schuyler continued:

> If such a number cannot be raised out of the said Indians, that the companies be completed with white men living in the vicinity of the said Indians and accustomed to the woods, provided that the white men do not exceed in number one-third of the Indians. That the pay, provisions and billet money be the same as is now given to the troops in the service of the United Colonies. That such as cannot furnish their own arms be supplied out of the public store, paying for them out of their wages. That the Committee at Stockbridge and Mr. Edwards is requested to apppoint such officers

for the Stockbridge company, either of white men or Indians, as they shall deem best qualified for the service.

Washington received this Resolution from Schuyler on 21 June in a detailed twelve-page letter. In it the Albany general also announced the Commissioners' further attempt to counteract traditional British influence by calling for a conference with the Six Nations at German Flats, a traditional Native American meeting ground sixty-five miles northwest of the city. Perhaps nervous at the celerity of his actions, Schuyler disarmingly added: "I am happy I have anticipated your Excellency's advice to convene the Indians."

Could Schuyler have anticipated Washington's dismay? The commander who had been pleading that "the situation of our affairs will not suffer further delay," was apparently quite surprised to learn of his subordinate's haste in soliciting the available Stockbridge veterans—from a location deep within Revolutionary territory—for further Continental Army service. Everyone, it seemed, including Washington and the Congress, had been thinking and talking about enlisting only "border Indians."

How had the confusion arisen? And why did the commander in chief avoid shouldering responsibility for an action he himself had initiated and urged on a subordinate? Was there vacillation in the heart and mind of this man who had once come close to losing his life in a French-led ambush by Native Americans in the forests of western Pennsylvania? Was this another side to Washington, alluded to years later in a New England newspaper?[11]

Attempting some explanation to Hancock and Congress, Washington—who, with three secretaries, maintained the most voluminous correspondence of any general in history—dashed off an immediate apology. In a turnabout somewhat less than complete, he wrote on 21 June 1776:

> The Commissioners of Indian Affairs, at a meeting in Albany in consequence of the Resolutions of Congress (as they say) which I transmitted June 7th, for engaging Indians in our service, appear to me to have widely mistaken the views of Congress in this

[11] *The New Hampshire Gazette*, 4 March 1780, quoted "an American gentleman now in London" on the commander in chief's "utter aversion to all Indians."

instance, and to have formed a plan for engaging such Indians as were not in contemplation.

Writing thusly, Washington avoided the fact that twice within the previous fortnight he himself had urged on Schuyler the need for an immediate conference with the Six Nations. With no apparent embarrassment, he continued, "I cannot account on what principles they have gone," Washington, eventually mythologized for his reluctance to bend the truth, continued, "as a part of their proceedings show they are about to hold a conference with the Six Nations." In the throes of a desperate Revolutionary struggle whose fundamental document would affirm the equality of mankind, Washington's view on the native population of the North American continent was curiously ambivalent. But conscience forced the commander in chief to add, however weakly, "I suppose they esteemed what they have done a necessary measure."

Three days later, Washington assumed a more diplomatic tone with Schuyler, giving no hint of his previous comments to Hancock and the Congress:

> In respect to the proceedings of the Commissioners for raising two companies of Mohikander Indians, they appear to me not to answer the views of Congress. Congress's design was extended to those Indians who were not livers among us, but were of hostile character and doubtful friendship. But in this I may be mistaken, and there may be a necessity of engaging those you have, to secure their interest.

Washington correctly understood the uproar Schuyler's action was creating in Philadelphia. On 24 June, Congress, dreading the idea of arming "local savages" resolved "that a letter be written to General Washington desiring him to put a stop to the raising of the companies of Mohickan and Stockbridge Indians." Hancock immediately transmitted these instructions to the commander in chief, adding:

> The Commissioners have undoubtedly mistaken the intention of Congress, although the terms in which the Resolution was conceived may at first view seem to give a latitude of construction to the place in which the Indians are to be raised. I request that you

give orders to have a stop put to raising the Mohickan and Stockbridge Indians as soon as possible.

Presumably to mollify Schuyler, Hancock also approved a legalism, suggested by Washington's report, to avoid the Albany general's unanticipated recruiting of local natives proving an embarrassment to Connecticut's Governor Jonathan Trumbull, since the Stockbridge area of Massachusetts was within his military jurisdiction.

That same day, as the first vessels of a huge British invasion fleet dropped anchor in New York's Lower Bay, Washington—always capable of administering a thousand agonizing details at once—found time to write this to Schuyler:

> Congress having disapproved the proceedings of the Commissioners at Albany on June 13th so far as they relate to raising two companies of Mohekan and Stockbridge Indians, I request you to put the most early and speedy stop to the same.

The commander in chief was still strangely unwilling to accept major responsibility for putting Philip Schuyler in the Congressional doghouse:

> The Honorable President observes in his letter that the Resolve for employing Indians is conceived in such terms as to give at first view a latitude of construction as to the place in which they are to be raised, and the Commissioners must have understood it so, which led to the mistake.

Did Washington realize that only two Commissioners, Douw and Schuyler, were involved in this "mistake"? If so, his letter was extremely conciliatory.

THE WAR was now riding at anchor off New York City, and the British had begun to ferry their 22,000 regulars and Hessian mercenaries ashore on Staten Island. On 4 July, the possibility of augmenting the vastly outnumbered Revolutionary forces with Native American volunteers resurfaced—on a new front. With Schuyler's Continentals now in full flight from Canada (and subordinate General Horatio Gates quarreling with Schuyler over departmental command), Connecticut Governor Trumbull wrote anxiously to Washington:

> The retreat of the Northern Army and its situation have spread a
> general alarm, exposing the frontiers of New York and New
> Hampshire. Some settlements, I am informed, are breaking up and
> removing.

The commander in chief promptly recalled Hancock's year-old attempt to recruit Native American nations on the northeastern frontier to defend the Canadian border, and suggested to Philadelphia: "It may now be agreeable to engage the St. John's, Nova Scotia, and Penobscot Indians in our favor. I have been told that several, perhaps five or six hundred or more, might be got to join us."

Congress quickly approved that demonstration of concern for the country's borders. On 8 July, the legislators resolved that Washington might request Massachusetts ". . .to call forth and engage in the service of the United States so many Indians of the St. John's, Nova Scotia and Penobscot tribes as he shall judge necessary." Three days later, Washington advised Hancock he was asking for ". . .five or six hundred of them to be enlisted for two or three years if they will consent to it."

With that request, military expediency bridged a 150-year-old cultural gap: on the frontier at least, Native Americans were formally welcomed as soldiers in the American Army. But Washington, in his appeal to the Massachusetts legislature, showed his welcome to be not unconditional. He wrote:

> Having professed a strong inclination to take part with us in the
> present contest, it is probable that these tribes may be engaged for
> less pay and upon better terms than the Continental troops.

By August, the British disembarkation on Staten Island was complete. The enemy stood ready to strike across New York Bay at what had become the most strategically important city in the new "United States." Washington nervously reminded Massachusetts that he had ". . .heard nothing from them. It is a matter of the greatest consequence, and I must therefore beg an answer."

Meanwhile, the natives of Stockbridge, puzzled and offended by Schuyler's abrupt turnabout and knowing nothing of the correspondence passing between him, Washington, and Hancock, decided to act on their own. Aware of the danger threatening New York City, they sent representatives to plead with the commander in chief to allow them to participate in its defense. Washington wrote to Hancock:

> I am informed by General Putnam that there are some Stockbridge Indians here (I have not seen them myself) who profess great uneasiness at their not being employed by us, and have come to inquire into the cause.

With the powerful British fleet lying in the harbor, there was a discernible shift in tone in Washington's reassurance to Hancock in Philadelphia:

> I am sensible Congress had them [the Stockbridges] not in contemplation when they resolved that Indians might be engaged in our service. However, they seem anxious, as they were led to expect it from what General Schuyler and the other Commissioners did.

Then, underlining the presence of a powerful enemy force less than ten miles away, Washington continued:

> As we are under difficulties in getting men, and there may be danger of the Indians, or some of them, taking an unfavourable part, I beg leave to submit to Congress as my opinion under all these circumstances, that they had better be employed.

(At that very moment, the War Office in London was weighing an identical suggestion, carried in a letter from "A Soldier of the American Indian Wars," stressing the skills in warfare of Native Americans and suggesting that:

> . . .employing a body of Indians in our Army would be attended with many and great advantages, securing the troops from all kinds of surprizes by scouring the woods for many miles around and giving timely notice of any danger before it arrived. No one who has not been in America can conceive with what swiftness the Indians scamper through the woods, and with what certainty they can distinguish objects at a considerable distance.)

In the growing military crisis—an unnerving defeat in the north and a huge enemy force threatening the defenses of New York City—the mood of Congress was rapidly changing; discrimination against friendly native volunteers had become impractical. On 2 August, the delegates in Philadelphia set forth the following: "...Resolved, That General Washington be instructed to employ in the service of the States, as many of the Stockbridge Indians as he shall judge proper."

Hancock passed on the word that same day: "The Congress approve of your employing in the service of the States the Stockbridge Indians, if you think it proper." The commander in chief immediately wrote to the natives' delegate to the Massachusetts Congress, Timothy Edwards,[12] who had been shuttling between Albany and Stockbridge. Washington's letter was the epitome of Southern courtesy:

> The enclosed copy of a Resolution of Congress, entered into August 2nd, will discover to you their sentiments on the subject of employing Stockbridge Indians in the service of the United States. It is certain they differed some time ago from the Commissioners of Indian Affairs and put a stop to their proceedings in this instance. But finding that our enemies are prosecuting the war with unexampled severity and industry, and that these Indians are anxious to take a part in our favour, they have instructed me to employ in the service of the American States as many of them as I think proper. I therefore take the liberty to request your friendly exertions on this occasion, and that you will engage in the service as many of them as you possibly can. . .
>
> I would wish that you would give the whole of them, or any part that may choose it, the liberty of joining this army, or that in the Northern Department under General Schuyler. I do not think it will be proper, as they are desirious of becoming a part of the army, to oblige them to join where they have not an inclination to go; and therefore recommend that they should be indulged in whatever way their fancy may lead, as to joining either one or the other army, partially or wholly. The situation of our affairs will readily suggest to you the necessity of dispatch. At the same time, it will point out the expediency of engaging as many of them as

---

[12] Edwards would be elected the following year as a Massachusetts delegate to the Continental Congress.

you can. The business may be attended with a degree of trouble, which I could wish not to happen, but yet I am persuaded it will be undertaken with alacrity.

Washington had already sent this message to Edwards when two of the Stockbridge natives already in New York City visited his headquarters. The commander in chief received them formally, and presently sent them away bearing a second letter to Edwards:

This will be delivered to you by Samuel and John, two of our friends of the Stockbridge Indians, who have been here and expressed the desire of their people to become part of the Army of the United States. Having wrote you fully on August 7th and transmitted a copy of the Resolution of the Congress upon this subject (which I presume will have reached you before this comes to hand), I have referred them to you for information in the instance of their application. I request the favor of your early attention to what I recommended to your care and direction.

It took three weeks for Washington to receive a reply from Edwards, who was busy elsewhere:

Upon my return from the Treaty at the German-Flats on August 17th,[13] I communicated the contents of your letters of August 7th and 10th to the Indians of this place then at hand. On August 23rd, being generally collected from their various dispersions, they resolved to join the Army under General Schuyler, and the main body of them propose to march tomorrow. As some are still at their hunting and fishing grounds, the number that will engage cannot be ascertained.

Possibly tongue in cheek, Edwards added:

General Schuyler has doubtless informed Your Excellency that, as you had been silent about the terms and mode of engaging them, he advised me to execute the plan adopted by the Commissioners of Indian Affairs for this Department last June, a copy of

[13] This, at long last, was the Six Nations Conference of the Iroquois, an attempt to neutralize British political and military influence on the New York and Pennsylvania frontiers. It had been quickly convened by the Commissioners for Indian Affairs after the shift in Congressional opinion. "This is a family quarrel between you and

which was then sent you. This I have followed. Any services which
I can execute, you may be assured shall be undertaken with alacrity.

Within a week, two companies of Native American and white
troops were on the march together from Stockbridge through the
upper Hudson Valley, to help stem Sir Guy Carleton's invasion
down from Canada.
It was critical that the Revolutionary army be able to distinguish
their new recruits from Carleton's "skulking Indian allies." Until
some form of Continental uniform could be procured from the
quartermaster's supply, Washington's General Orders cautioned:

> The Indians are severally to wear a blue and red cap, as a distin-
> guishing mark. Of this, all officers and soldiers are to take particular
> notice, to the end that we may not by mistake kill our friends
> instead of our foes.

Washington himself had learned to distinguish friends from foes.

old England," said Abraham, chief sachem of the Upper Mohawks, "Our resolution
to sit still and see you both fight it out is not to be broken."
    But it was indeed broken the following year by secret ministerial negotiations
during a London visit by another devout Christianized Mohawk leader, Joseph Brant
(Thayendanegea), the half-brother of Sir William Johnson's vivacious concubine,
Molly Brant. Joseph Brant, one of the most remarkable figures in 18th-century
American history, was a thoughtful and brave Mohawk of mixed blood, a Johnson
protégé, and a lionized visitor to Great Britain; he moved easily through English and
colonial social circles.
    When not traveling among the Iroquois nations, Brant raised horses and cattle.
He lived with his family in a frame house on a farm near Canajoharie, forty miles
northwest of Albany. Brant viewed with alarm the pressures of colonial immigration
to the western New York and Pennsylvania frontiers and, in the end, was able to
hold all but the Iroquois Oneida nation to the historic connection with Great Britain,
and helped lead the native opposition to Sullivan's punitive expedition in 1779 (see
Chapter XI).
    But the young Stockbridge representative at the German Flats conference,
Captain Hendricks Solomon, made his group's political orientation very clear. He
told the Commissioners: "Depend on it. We are true to you and mean to join you."
Chief Solomon declared, "Our bones shall die with yours. We are determined never
to be at peace with the Redcoats while they are at variance with you. If we are
conquered, our lands go with yours. If you are victorious, we hope you will help us
recover our just rights." Years later, Brant would characterize Solomon as a "Yankee
Indian."

CHAPTER III

# Spy in the Ointment

*IN WHICH a brilliant young New Englander, destined for fame as one of Europe's great scientists, infamously betrays his own country.*

*FOR SEVERAL WEEKS* in the fall of 1775, an enemy spy wandered in and out of the Continental Army installations at Cambridge. The spy looked like any other young American recruit, but his mind was racing feverishly as his penetrating eye recorded signs of weakness in the Revolutionaries' organization. And there were many. His observations produced a detailed written report that encouraged British hopes that American morale would soon collapse, bringing the Revolution to an inglorious end. This turncoat was Benjamin Thompson of Woburn, Massachusetts, and Concord (once called Rumford), New Hampshire. Rather than meeting a traitor's bitter and ignoble end, Thompson was just beginning what was to become a brilliant career.

Always a go-getter, three years before the Revolution this Massachusetts farm boy married a wealthy New Hampshire widow fourteen years his senior and moved to Concord, sixty miles north of Woburn on the Merrimack River. There he enjoyed her "competent Estate."

Through the new Mrs. Thompson, the young man became a confidant of the ardent royalist governor of New Hampshire Colony, John Wentworth. The latter soon angered the members of his 15th Regiment of Militia by making the inexperienced Thompson a provincial officer with the rank of major.

In December 1774, as Revolutionary tempers began to rise throughout New England, Thompson was summoned before the

Concord Committee of Correspondence[1] to answer allegations that
he was "a Rebel to the State, and unworthy of the benefits of Civil
Society." He was acquitted for lack of evidence.

Leaving Mrs. Thompson behind in Concord, the covert Tory
fled across the colony's border into Massachusetts. He never saw his
wife again, and thereafter tried to keep his whereabouts a secret from
her. She died in Concord in 1793.

After the battles of Lexington and Concord, Massachusetts,
Thompson attempted to scheme his way to being named a Continental officer—for what purpose only he knew. He was rebuffed, both
because of his youth and his poorly concealed royalist sympathies.

In May 1775, smarting from a brief imprisonment by the
Woburn Committee of Correspondence based on fresh allegations
that Thompson was "enemical to the Liberties of this Country," he
assumed the guise of a New England militiaman. As such, he would
have access to secret American defense information he intended to
feed to Sir William Howe, the new British commander in Boston.

Thompson's espionage report of 4 November 1775 to the British,
injudiciously if boldly signed "B.T." (if traced to Thompson by the
Americans, he would have been hanged), conveyed data vital to the
enemy, describing the shortages, illnesses, and lack of discipline
plaguing the infant American army. It bears examination in detail,
because no other firsthand written account from either side so
candidly pictures the perilous state of the Revolutionary fighting
force.

Thompson entitled his secret report to Lord Howe, "Miscel-
lanius Observations on the state of the Rebel Army." Besides analyz-
ing the difficult problems facing the Revolutionary army, Thompson
is most specific about the Continentals' available arms and ammunition. No dilettante spy, he minutely described the storage sites for
the modest but invaluable quantities of American gunpowder.
Thompson begins by assessing a possible amphibious attack on
Boston:

> Upon Sunday October 15th I saw the flat-bottom'd boats or
> Batteaus lying just below Cambridge Bridge, & two more were
> making in the yard— The workmen informed me that one was
> finished every day, and that more workmen were daily expected

[1] The group included 23-year-old Henry Dearborn (see *Chapter XI*, note 2). 3 ( p 1 50)

from Newbury— These Boats are built of common deal Boards,
& in general will contain 50 to 60 Men, including the Rowers—
What number of them were to be made I could not learn.

It is generally supposed in the Rebel Army that an attack is
designed on either Charlestown or Boston, or both—and that these
boats are preparing to transport Troops to those places—but many
of the more intelligent, and among these some of their principal
Officers, rather suppose these preparations are only to amuse ye
Kings Troops, and by keeping them continually alarm'd with
apprehension of being attacked, prevent their going to distant parts
of the Country to Ravage—

About the 13th of October, a return was made of the number
of Men that all the boats of every denomination (exclusive of the
flat-bottom'd boats) in the Rebel Camp were capable of transport-
ing—and I was told by a Person who saw said Return that the total
number was 550—

Thompson's secret report moves on to discuss the Americans'
available gunpowder and the location of their critical magazines:

From the best information I have been able to get with respect to
their Military Stores, the total quantity of Gun Powder that they
have in their Camp (exclusive of what is distributed among the
Troops) may be somewhere between 12 and 15 Tons.

The only Magazines on the left wing of the army (that I know
of) are the Powder House, a round stone building about half or
three quarters of a Mile N.W. of Winter Hill, over which a
Subalterns Guard mounts—and a small cave in the W. side of
Prospect Hill, the entrance to which is defended by a small Trench
& parapet which descends obliquely from the Fort down the side
of the hill.

This magazine is inaccessible from without on account of the
steepness of the hill on the W. side, but I apprehend that if a Party
could by any means come in upon the rear of their encampment,
the Powder House might very easily be surprized as it is at a very
considerable distance from any of their Works and is defended but
by a small party. What quantity of Gun Powder is contained in
these two Magazines I have not been able to learn.

On the N.W. side of Cambridge Common is the Laboratory
[for making gunpowder] round which two or three Companies are
encamp'd. But I believe no considerable quantity of Powder is ever
kept in this place nor at any other place at or near Cambridge.

In Watertown at the distance of about half a mile N. from the meeting house is a School house which I am told is one of their principal Magazines of Gun Powder—The Company in Watertown furnish a Guard for it, and two Centries are constantly planted here in the daytime and four on the Night.

There was a house about halfway from Cambridge to Watertown in which a considerable quantity of Powder was lodged about 3 months ago over which a strong Guard was mounted, but I believe it has since been removed to Prospect & Winter Hill Magazines, 'tho I am not absolutely certain of it.

As to the quantity of Powder and the situation of the Magazines upon the right wing of the Army, I have never been able to get any satisfactory accounts. I was lately told that a small regular square Redoubt which has been erected upon a very considerable eminence in the back part of Roxbury was built to defend a grand Magazine which was to be erected there, but I rather suppose it is designed and built to command the Town and their other Works, which it is very well calculated to do.

Thompson's report continues with an evaluation of the American artillery train:

As to Shot I believe the Rebels are in want of no kind of it as large quantities of it of every sort have lately been cast in the Country, and the Furnaces are still employed in that service.

Their Canon in general are excessively bad—many of which that are mounted and planted are intirely useless. 12 pieces of 18 and 24 pounders which came from the Fort at Newport are really much more valuable than every piece of ordnance they have in their Camp. But they are not anxious to increase the quantity of their Artilery till they can have some certainty of a supply of Gun Powder which at present I believe they have not.

Thompson discusses the Americans' arms and ammunition:

Their Fire Arms in general are but very indifferent and I believe two thirds of their Pieces are destitute of Bayonets—But there is a great number of Armourers in the Camp, who are constantly employed in making good these deficiencies—The Pieces in general are owned by the Soldiers and are re-filled at the expence of the Colonies.

Exclusive of 25 or 30 rounds of Cartridge & Ball which each
Soldier has in his Cartouch Box, they have lately had a pound of
Buck Shot served out to each man to keep loose in his pocket, and
make use of occasionally—and I am told that every soldier in the
Camp is soon to be supplied with an additional 60 rounds of
Cartridges which are to be carried in a leather bag made for that
purpose, and hung over the right shoulder by a strap—
    The Officers are universally armed with a Musquet and Bayo-
net and some few of them have added a Sword. They are also
supposed to carry a Pike or Espantoon. I have never seen in their
Camp, and believe they make no use at all of these Weapons.[2]

Presumably to make it easy for the King's soldiers to pick off
Continental officers, Thompson carefully describes their symbols of
rank:

The marks of distinction among them are as follows, Viz—the
Commander in chief wears a wide blue ribbond between his Coat
and waist-Coat, over the right shoulder and across the breast—
Major Generals a Pink Ribbond in the same manner—Brigadier
Generals a [word left blank] Ribbond—and all Aids du Camp a
green one—all Field Officers wear Red, Pink, or scarlett Cockades—Captains Yellow or Buff Cockades and Subalterns Green
ones—

He describes the passages into the American fortifications:

Their Works in general are very extensive, and as strong as Labour
alone can make them, but Engineers are very much wanted in their
Camp—
    The entrance or passage-way into their Forts & Redoubts are
all defended by Traverses, and in general there is a plank Bridge
over the ditch which is drawn up & fastened by Chains to two
posts even with the external face of the Parapet—Which Bridges,
drawn up, intirely closes the passage into the Fort or Redoubt. And

---

[2] A general shortage of firearms led to Washington's order that his infantry officers
revive the outmoded European military custom of carrying semi-ceremonial hal-
berds—a combination spear and battle-axe. Such pikes were both marks of rank and
useful defense weapons for close quarters. Pike-carrying rapidly fell into disuse in
the American army, before it could be proved in serious hand-to-hand combat.

where they have no Bridges, the entrances are defended by Cheveau de frize.

Thompson looks askance at the American soldiers' battle dress:

The Army in general is not only badly accoutered, but most retchedly cloathed and as dirty a set of mortals as ever disgraced the name of a Soldier— They have had no Clothes of any sort provided for them by the Congress (except the detachment of 1133 that are gone to Canada under Col. [Benedict] Arnold, who had a new coat and a linen frock served out to each of them before they sat out). Tho the Army in general, and the Massachusetts forces in particular, had encouragement of having Coats given them by way of bounty for inlisting— And the neglect of the Congress to fulfill their promise in this respect has been a source of not a little uneasiness among the Soldiers.

They have no Women in the Camp to do washing for the men, and they in general not being used to doing things of this sort, and thinking it rather a disparagement to them, choose rather to let their linen &c rot upon their backs than to be at the trouble of cleaning 'em themselves. And to this nasty way of life, and to the change of their diet from milk, vegetables &c to living almost intirely upon Flesh, must be attributed those Putrid, Malignant, and infectious disorders which broke out among them soon after their taking the field, and which have prevailed with unabating fury during the whole summer.

Thompson describes the unhealthy character of the American encampment:

The leading men among them (with their usual art & cunning) have been indefatigable in their indeavours to conceal the real State of the Army in this respect, and to convince the World that the Soldiers were tolerably healthy. But the contrary has been apparent, even to a demonstration to every Person that has had but the smallest acquaintance with their Camp— And so great was the prevalence of these disorders in the month of July, that out of 4207 men who were stationed upon Prospect Hill, no more than 2227 were returned fit for duty—

The mortallity among them must have been very great, and to this in a great measure must be attributed the present weakness of their Regiments, many of which were much stronger when they came into the Field— But the number of Soldiers that have died in the Camp is comparatively small to those vast numbers that have gone off in the interior parts of the Country: For immediately upon being taken down with these disorders they have in general been carried back into the Country to their own homes, where they have not only died themselves, but by spreading the infection among their Relations & Friends have introduced such a general mortallity throughout New England as was never known since its first planting— Great numbers have been carried off in all parts of the Country—some Towns 'tis said have lost near one third of their inhabitants, and there is scarce a Village in New England but has suffer'd more or less from the raging virulence of these dreadful disorders—

Perhaps the intolerable heats and continual drought during the late summer, by inclining the Blood to a putrid state, and rendering it more easily susceptible of the infection, may have contributed not a little to the spread of these diseases—

He describes shortages of food and other necessities:

Every article of provision that is the natural produce of the Country is extreamly cheap in the Camp; except the article Bread, which is very far from being easily available, as the price of Corn of every sort is much raised, on account of a very great scarsity of it, occasioned by the late drought— Rye which used commonly to be Sold at 2/3 and 2/6, is now sold in many places at 4/ & 4/6 pr Bushel, and every other sort of grain in proportion. But the army expect to be supplied from the Southward—

The best of fresh Beef is now sold at one penny three farthings pr lb—and good Mutton from three half-pence to two pence pr lb. But nothwithstanding, fresh Provisions are cheap and plenty, yet I have heard of no considerable magazines that are forming—

Many Capital Medicines are not to be bought in the Country—and in general those that are to be had are at an advanc'd price of 5 or 600 pr Cent— The price of West India Goods is rais'd in general from 70 to 100 pr Cent— English Goods about as much (notwithstanding a resolve of Congress to the contrary), and Irish Linens are not to be bought at any price.

The reason why fresh provisions of every sort are so remark- ably plenty, is the universal scarsity of Hay throughout the Country, occasioned by the late drought. The want of which article is so great that the farmers in general cannot possibly keep more than

two thirds of their usual quantity of stock alive during the Winter— And if they do not kill them this Fall, many of them must
unvoidably perish by famine— But tho' this circumstance may
make Provisions extreamly cheap and plenty this Year, yet it
cannot fail to have a very different effect upon the next.

The American soldiers' morale, Thompson insists, is low—and
sinking lower:

The Soldiers in general are most heartily sick of the service, and I
believe it would be with the utmost difficulty that they could be
prevailed upon to serve another Campaign— The Continental
Congress are very sensible of this and have lately sent a Committee
to the Camp to consult with the General officers upon some
method of raising the necessary forces to serve during the Winter
Season, as the greatest part of the Army that is now in the field is
to be disbanded upon the last day of December—
    Whether they will be successful in their indeavours to per-
swade the Soldiers to re-inlist, or not, I cannot say, but am rather
inclined to think that they will, For as they are men posess'd of
every species of cunning and artifice, and as their Political existance
depends upon the existance of the Army, they will leave no stone
unturn'd to accomplish their designs—

Thompson feels the egalitarian army has gone too far. When it
comes to democracy, Thompson—and later, Count Rumford—just
doesn't get it:

Notwithstanding the indefatigable indeavours of Mr. Washington
and the other Generals, and particularly of Adjutant General
Gates, to arrange and discipline the Army, yet any tolerable degree
of Order and Subordination is what they are totally unacquainted
with in the Rebel Camp. And the doctrines of independence &
levellism have been so effectually sown throughout the Country
and so universally imbibed by all ranks of men, that I apprehend
it will be with the greatest difficulty that the inferior Officers, and
Soldiers, will be ever brought to any tolerable degree of subjection
to the commands of their Superiors.
    Many of their leading men are not insensible of this, and I have
often heard them lament that the existance of that very Spirit which
induced the common People to take up Arms and resist the
authority of Great Britain, should induce them to reject the author-

ity of their own Officers, and by that means effectually prevent their ever making good Soldiers.

Another great reason why it is impossible to introduce a proper degree of subordination in the Rebel Army, is the great degree of equallity as to birth, fortune and education that universally prevails among them. For men cannot bear to be commanded by others that are their superiors in nothing but in having had the good fortune to get a Superior Commission, for which perhaps they stood equally fair. And in addition to this the Officers and men are not only in general very nearly upon par as to birth, fortune &c— but in particular Regiments are most commonly neighbours and acquaintances & as such can with less Patience submit to that degree of absolute submission and Subordination which is necessary to form a well disciplined corps.

Thompson feels that dissension between troops from different states will be inevitable:

Another reason why the army can never be well united and regulated is the disagreement and jealousies between the different Troops from the different Colonies, which must ever create disaffection and uneasiness among them. The Massachustts forces already complain very loudly of the partiallity of the General to the Virginians, and have even gone so far as to tax him with taking pleasure in bringing their Officers to Court Martials, and having them Cashired that he may fill their places with his friends from that quarter— The Gentlemen from the Southern Colonies, in their turn complain of the enormous proportion of New England Officers in the Army, and particularly of those belonging to the province of Massachusetts Bay, and say as the cause is now become a common one and the expence is general, they ought to have equal chance for Command with their neighbours.[3]

Thus have these jealousies and uneasiness already begun which I think cannot fail to increase, and grow every day more and more interesting, and if they do not finally destroy the very existance of the Army (which I think they bid very fair to do) it must unavoid-

---

[3] Thompson was right about inherent state rivalries. Even Washington was forced to exhort his troops "that the honour and success of the Army, and the safety of your bleeding Country, depends on your harmony and good agreement with each other, with all distinction sunk in the name of 'an American.' "

ably render it much less formidable than it otherways might have been.

Thompson particularly deprecates the boisterous conduct of the elite young Virginia riflemen, whose deadly accurate home-bored weapons carried 150 paces beyond the range of the best of the thirteen varieties of muskets used by the rest of the army:

> Of all useless sets of men that ever incumbered an Army, surely the boasted Rifle-men are certainly the most so— When they came to Camp they had every Liberty and indulgence allow'd that they could possibly wish for— They had more pay than any other soldiers—did no duty—were under no restraint from the commands of their Officers, but went when & where they pleased, without being subject to be stopped or examined by any one, and did almost intirely as they pleased in every respect whatever—But they have not answered the end for which they were designed in any one article whatever. For instead of being the best marksmen in the World, and picking off every Regular that was to be seen, there is scarsely a Regiment in Camp but can produce men that can beat them at Shooting— and the Army is universally convinced that the continual fire which they kept up by the Week and Month together has had no other effect than to waste their amunition, and convince the King's Troops that they are not really so formidable adversaries as they would wish to be thought—
> Mr. Washington is very sensible of this, and has not only strictly forbid them passing the advanced Centries to fire at the Kings Troops, without particular Orders for that purpose, but has lately obliged them to do duty as other Troops. And to be sure there never was a more mutinous and undisciplined set of Villains that bred disturbance in any Camp.
> The whole number of these men in the Camp may be somewhere about 650—and I believe the total number of Troops of every denomination in the Army including Officers is very near upon 15000—
> ----*Boston 4th November 1775*
> B.T.

It is interesting that this exhaustive betrayal came not from some powdered parvenu, like Benedict Arnold's infamous co-conspirator, Major John André, but from a perceptive and deceptive twenty-two-year-old schoolmaster whose ancestors had landed on New England shores only ten years after the Pilgrims.

The material Benjamin Thompson collected and privily conveyed to British headquarters across the Charles River provides a striking example of the dangers of combining espionage with wishful thinking. From his report, the Boston spymasters drew strategically inappropriate conclusions about patriot morale from wholly accurate information about troubles in the typhoid-wracked American camp.

Thompson's careful analysis offers an unusually vivid view of the various organizational shortcomings that beset the early American army. But for all its detail, the report proved of slight advantage to Thompson's British contacts, for he had discounted one factor, the most important of all. From "B.T.'s" earliest days in New Hampshire, he had unabashedly sought wealth, rank, and power. He had no problem recognizing and accomodating authority, but he was completely unable to discern, understand, or objectively report on the true secret weapon of the Revolutionary soldiers—a tenacious, unquenchable desire to be their own economic and political masters. Meanwhile, Thompson enjoyed his own heady freedom, the peculiar freedom of being a secret outsider.

Even in its bleakest moments, the Continental Army survived "B.T.'s" direst predictions. Despite his adroit espionage, the British were unable to break through the patriot ring around Boston. Eventually the enemy was forced to evacuate the city, taking with them their loyal agent Benjamin Thompson.

THE ERSTWHILE SPY was soon active on other fronts. Within two years, he was elected a Fellow of London's Royal Society. For a year, he served as Undersecretary of State for the Colonies, carrying on with Prime Minister Lord George Germain what 18th-century London gossips characterized as a "scandalous intimacy."

In 1781, the expatriate actually returned to British North America at the head of his own "regiment of horse"—the King's American Dragoons. On the very day Thompson's transport, blown off course, landed in Charleston, South Carolina, all his Massachusetts properties were finally confiscated by the Commonwealth.

Thompson's post-Revolutionary life is not without interest. When he left England for the European Continent a year after the war, it was to become Chamberlain to Duke Carl Theodor, Elector of Bavaria. In Munich, Thompson created for his royal master a huge public park, still called "The English Garden." He also successfully introduced productive workhouses, to reduce beggary. He reorganized Bavaria's military establishment, eventually serving as the country's Superintendent of Police and as its Minister of War.

In 1790, he was ennobled by the Elector of Bavaria as "Imperial Count Rumford of the Holy Roman Empire." Although Thompson was still a British subject, the Elector endeavored to have him accredited as Bavarian Ambassador to the Court of St. James. That was too much for King George III, who "decisively Objected."

All the while, Thompson's ardor for scientific research never dimmed. The young man who had begun his career counting Boston invasion boats was now developing heat convection theories that soon were improving smoky 18th-century fireplaces and kitchen stoves. He invented superior cooking utensils, including the drip coffee pot, designed more efficient lamps and carriage wheels, and conducted studies of heat and light. Thompson overturned the "caloric" concept of heat by properly identifying heat as a form of motion.

Knighted by his king at the tender age of thirty-one, Sir Benjamin was soon showered with honors as one of the world's most inventive research scientists. Continuing to appropriate additional titles and to dissemble about his origins (once suggesting to a French biographer that Rumford was a "little island between New-Hampshire and Massachusetts"), Thompson helped establish the Royal Institution, one of the world's preeminent scientific organizations, and for many years was active in its affairs. In 1802, after countless liasons all over Europe, he was married a second time, to the wealthy widow of the famous French scientist Lavoisier. Within a year Thompson was referring to his new wife as a "female Dragon."

Thompson became a military figure of such reknown that even so feisty a nationalist as John Adams importuned him to come home and serve as chief artillery instructor at a new United States military academy. The invitation deliberately turned a blind eye to Thompson's sorry record during the closing months of the Revolution, when he served in both South Carolina and New York as a Lieutenant Colonel in the British cavalry regiment he helped to raise. Thompson nevertheless showed his appreciation for the offer to let bygones be bygones by forwarding a model of a piece of field artillery he himself had designed. The Massachusetts Historical Society elected him to membership. Thompson evenhandedly gave $5,000 to both the Royal Society and the newly formed American Academy of Arts and Sciences, which then elected him an Honorary Foreign Member. He offered to underwrite awards from both groups for important discoveries concerning heat and light. Since then, the Academy's "Rumford Premium" has been awarded to (besides Thompson himself) a host of American scientific luminaries, including Ericsson, Langley, Edison, Langmuir, Compton, and Shapley.

Like some early Philip Nolan, the "Man Without a Country," Thompson never fully abandoned the possibility of one day returning to the country he had betrayed and abandoned. In a 1798 letter (now in Boston's American Academy of Arts and Sciences), the expatriate describes his dream of some

> little quiet retreat in the Country. . .from 1 to 4 miles from Cambridge. . .to which I can retire at some future period, and spend the evening of life. As I am not wealthy and prefer comfort to splendour. . .I should want nothing from the land but pleasure grounds, and grass for my Cows and Horses, and an extensive Kitchen Garden and fruit Garden. I should wish much for a few acres of wood, and for a stream of fresh water. . . for without shady Trees and water there can be no rural beauty.

NOTHING EVER CAME of this former dragoon colonel's idyllic dream of hearth and home. Thompson eventually left his French wife and settled in the Paris suburb of Auteuil, where he continued his laboratory experiments. He died in 1814 of a "nervous fever." Most of his estate was bequeathed to Harvard College—site of the Cambridge gunpowder "Laboratory" he had once pinpointed for the king's troops. The college subsequently set up the "Rumford Professorship of the Physical and Mathematical Sciences as Applied to the Useful Arts."

Thompson's acquaintance Baron Georges Cuvier, secretary to the Paris Academy of Sciences, read a eulogy at a meeting of the Academy in 1815: "He earned for himself both the esteem of the wise, and the gratitude of the unfortunate." The great French naturalist continued:

However, it was as if, while rendering all these valuable services to his fellow-men, he had no real love or regard for them. He thought it neither wise nor good to entrust to men in the mass the care of their own well-being. That right, which seems so natural to them, of judging whether they are wisely governed, appeared to him to be only a fictitious fancy born of false notions of enlightenment.

Three decades later, an American historian underlined Thompson's indecent behavior while a British cavalry colonel on Long Island: "His inexcusable acts gave him an immortality in this community that all his philosophical disquisitions and scientific discoveries could never secure to him."

The bones of Benjamin Thompson, Count Rumford—famous American experimenter who was ready to suffocate the American social experiment in its cradle—lie in a cemetery at Auteuil, in a grave still tended by the American Academy of Arts and Sciences and Harvard College.

# CHAPTER IV

# Two Battles on Harlem Heights

*IN WHICH Major André's long lost map finally resolves a battle royal over the site of a royal battle.*

*TURF IS* turf, especially among professional historians, who guard it zealously. From 1875 to 1883, the country's eight-year-long Centennial celebration of the Revolution offered plenty of time and opportunity for historians to develop some surprisingly bitter controversies about who did what to whom—and when and where. Clashing interpretations often pitted amateur and professional historians against each other. In the matter of choosing a site for the 100th anniversary celebration of New York City's Battle of Harlem Heights, the resultant historical free-for-all waxed almost as warm as the 18th-century military engagement itself.

The confrontation began innocently enough in the spring of 1876, when the New-York Historical Society decided to honor the clash of arms of 16 September 1776. A large outdoor celebration, including a picnic and orations by several prominent local historians, was planned on the battle site itself. It was the year after similar and very successful celebrations at Lexington and Concord.

Although the actual battle engaged fewer than a thousand troops on both sides, the seesaw military struggle on the rocky Heights (whose name was successively Vanderwater, Harlem, Bloomingdale, and, finally, Morningside) represented an important turning point in the early days of the Revolution. The battle ended with a clear-cut demonstration of the American army's strategic fighting ability. It also went far to vindicate the Congressional choice of George Washington as the Continental commander in chief. And, coming as it did on the heels of the disastrous rout of American troops on Long Island and their subsequent withdrawal from lower Manhattan, the victory on Harlem Heights went far to restore shattered Revolutionary confidence in their army's ability to stand up against the seasoned veterans of the British Crown.

The action of 16 September developed simply. In an early morning fog, a scouting party left the safety of the American lines on the high ground north of the "Hollow Way." This geographic feature was a deep valley at present-day West 125th Street that cut through the rocky ridge paralleling the Hudson River. The scouts were cautioned to precipitate no major action, but merely to determine for their commanding general how far the British had followed the American retreat of the previous day.

Letting down a few fence rails, the scouting party quickly crossed the Hollow Way and worked their way south onto higher ground. They moved cautiously through the drifting September morning fog until they came up against a British picket line near what is now West 108th Street.

After a brief skirmish, the Americans withdrew in good order, arriving back at the Hollow Way with two regiments of enemy Light Infantry in pursuit. Washington, correctly calculating that this British force was overextended, soon succeeded in luring it down off the ridge into the Hollow Way. At the same time, the commander in chief detached a well screened flanking column on a wide swing behind the enemy right. To insure the British remained engaged, Washington ordered a deliberately weak attack on the enemy front.

The battle was now fairly joined, but the American attack on the front proved far stronger than Washington intended. Instead of arriving at the enemy's rear, the circling Revolutionaries struck what an unexpected British retirement had turned into a well supported right flank.

In the shock of that contact, Lieutenant Colonel Thomas Knowlton—a thirty-five-year-old officer who had distinguished himself at Bunker Hill[1] by leading the Continental Army's first volunteer

---

[1] In one of John Trumbull's many iconic Revolutionary battle canvases, Knowlton was idealized as a huge man wearing a torn white shirt, dominating the foreground of the artist's "Battle of Bunker Hill."

commando unit, the Connecticut Rangers—was mortally wounded. In the days and months that lay ahead, Washington would sorely miss this intrepid Connecticut leader.

Few among the 17,000 Continentals under Washington's command possessed any sense of New York geography, so the bloody encounter on Harlem Heights soon became known among them simply as "Knowlton's battle," even though Knowlton fell early in the action.

As Knowlton's men deployed along the British right, his second in command, Virginian Major Andrew Leitch, was also hit. Carried from the field with ten other wounded Rangers, Leitch died the next day.

Uniting with the American force on the front, the Rangers were soon able to drive the formerly indomitable enemy into a field of ripening barley some distance to the south. It was here and in an adjoining peach orchard that the day's heaviest fighting swirled. In all, more than 225 American and British/German soldiers were killed or wounded.

Washington and the opposition's General Sir William Howe wanted to feel each other out. Neither cared nor was prepared to bring on a major conflict, although from time to time both fed a few fresh troops into the action. The Revolutionaries never lost their initial edge. By late afternoon, the disheveled British light infantry, despite German mercenary support, was back where it had started from in the morning. Fourteen of the British had been killed and a substantial number—154—wounded, compared with only forty wounded Americans. (They included Private Obadiah Brown from Gageborough, Massachusetts, of whom we shall hear more in *Chapters V* and *VI*.) Twenty Americans had been killed, most of them from the Connecticut Rangers. And Washington had lost a gallant and valuable field commander.

Considering "Knowlton's battle" won, the exhausted Revolutionary soldiers moved away in the gathering darkness. As they rested around their evening campfires north of Harlem Heights, they could savor their first taste of true battlefield victory since the militia triumph at Concord Bridge. They were exhilarated, with a new courage and determination. "Our men have recovered their spirits and feel a confidence which before they had quite lost," wrote Adjutant General Joseph Reed to his wife.

*THIS WAS* the hundred-year-old victory the good citizens of New York City gathered to celebrate on 16 September 1876. The New-York Historical Society assumed responsibility for the event, and its members began elaborate preparations:

> The ground was carefully studied by the committee charged with the details; all known maps, records, and deeds relating to the locality were examined and compared, and all the documents and letters, printed and in manuscript, known to exist, were collected and collated.[2]

The center of the battleground was finally determined to have been near the middle of Morningside Heights, near what is now Columbia University's Low Rotunda. We should note that apparently no contemporary maps were available that could pinpoint the location of the engagement. With the exception of the troops left in ill-fated Fort Washington, the Revolutionaries had abandoned New York City soon after the battle on 16 September, not to return there for seven years. There was no reason (or occasion) for them to map the site. The British, regarding the Battle of Harlem Heights as an "unfortunate skirmish," did not map it either. As far as the 1876 Committee could tell, the battle had not been formally located—except on a sketch map drawn by Sloss Hobart, a legislator who participated in the action. This map had been transcribed as an entry in the diary of the noted cleric Ezra Stiles, D.D.,[3] with the following notation:

> oct 18-1776—when I was at Fairfield I saw Sloss Hobart Esq a sensible Gent & a member of the New-York Convention. He gave me the following draft of the Action of 16 Sept which began near the 14 m stone & ended at the 8 m stone.[4]

---

[2] From the Centennial Address by John Jay III, U.S. Ambassador to Austria-Hungary.

[3] In 1778, Stiles became president of Yale College.

[4] These stone markers had been emplaced a dozen years earlier by Deputy Postmaster General Benjamin Franklin.

Stiles's milestone identifications were incorrect and contributed greatly to subsequent confusion. Even so, the outlines of Hobart's crude sketch easily fitted the battle site onto Morningside Heights.

Paragraphs from two contemporary letters served to corroborate the Committee's choice of Morningside. One letter was sent by New York Militia General George Clinton to his wife only a few days after the battle. He wrote, "Our Army, at least one division of it, lay at Colo. Morris's[5] & so southward to near the Hollow Way, which runs across from Harlem Flats to the North River and Matje Davit's Fly."[6]

This clearly identified the Hollow Way as the valley of present-day West 125th Street, for no other comparable geographic feature exists on upper-Manhattan.

Then, in a letter dated 18 September, Lewis Morris (who ten weeks earlier had put his name to the Declaration of Independence) wrote of the battle: ". . .the enemy advance to the top of the hill, which was opposite to that which lies before Dayes door."

The Day Tavern was located near present-day West 126th Street, on the main road leading out of New York City. Five miles north on this road, at the end of Manhattan Island, lay the King's Bridge[7] over Spuyten Duyvil Creek, across which Washington was soon forced to evacuate most of his army.

Directly across King's Bridge Road from the tavern, a steep slope led up to a narrow stone outcrop called "Point of Rocks." This point overlooked the Hollow Way, at the southernmost tip of the high ground on which the Revolutionary army was encamped. It was from Point of Rocks that Washington directed the course of the battle.

On these skimpy but reasonably conclusive bits of evidence, the Centennial Committee was content to locate the battle site near the precipitous eastern slope of Morningside Heights, a strip that is now Morningside Park, West 110th to 123rd Streets. A bunting-draped speakers' stand was erected near the edge of the rocky cliff up which Knowlton's flanking Rangers had supposedly clambered. It afforded a fine view of the many vegetable gardens in the Harlem valley below.

---

[5] The present-day Jumel Mansion at West 160th Street and Edgecombe Avenue that served as Washington's headquarters in September 1776.

[6] A swampy meadow at the edge of the Hudson.

[7] For several months in 1776, Revolutionary purists described this strategic span as "Congress Bridge," creating some confusion.

The celebration was held on a beautiful fall afternoon and proved
a thoroughly enjoyable event. The New-York Historical Society was
understandably proud of its work, and the group's distinguished
members closed the book on their research and preparation with a
feeling of great patriotic satisfaction.

BUT ONLY a year-and-a-half later, at the regular spring meeting of the
Society in February 1878, it became clear that grave doubts about the
Committee's discharge of its obligations had arisen in the mind of at
least one member. This was no less a personage than the Chancellor
of the University of the State of New York, the Honorable Erastus
C. Benedict. He delivered a paper, later privately printed as a sixty-
two-page booklet, wherein he charged the Celebration Committee
with gross negligence and hasty misinterpretation in selecting Morningside Heights as the battlefield site. Actually, claimed Chancellor
Benedict, the engagement was fought two miles to the north, in the
vicinity of what is now the museum complex at Audubon Terrace.
    A heated debate ensued, with Benedict, an amateur historian,
ranged against the entire vocal membership of the New-York Historical Society. The Chancellor's theory rallied no support.
    Benedict died two years later, but the dispute over the battlefield
site was destined to flare up again. With publication of Martha J. R.
N. Lamb's three-volume *History of the City of New York*, it became
apparent that, before his death, Benedict had succeeded in convincing
Mrs. Lamb, for she located the Hollow Way as "the ravine, now
Audubon Park [West 153rd to 155th Streets east of Riverside
Drive],"[8] and reiterated Benedict's arguments, adding a few interpretations of her own. Most surprising was that almost all the primary
sources used by Lamb (and earlier, by Benedict) to repudiate the
selection of Morningside Heights as the battlefield site were identical
with those previously presented by the Committee to support it. The
Stiles-Hobart map, with its milestone numbers, was one such source;
another was further quotation from the Clinton letter. Newly introduced by Lamb was a brief account by a British officer. Lamb's final
argument was that cannonballs had recently been unearthed near
Audubon Terrace.

---

[8] *History of the City of New York, Its Origin, Rise, and Progress*, vol. III.

If one were to accept the Hobart milestone numbers as accurate, the battle did indeed take place on (lower) Washington Heights. And the crossed swords on Hobart's map, by which he denoted Washington's command post on Point of Rocks, could be misinterpreted as representing the Morris (Jumel) Mansion (see footnote 5).

George Clinton's complete letter home had contained a brief account of the entire battle. In it, he estimated the various distances covered by the Americans on 16 September to total two and a half miles. This meant that, if the battle began at Morningside Heights, it would have ended at present-day West 75th Street, or a mile and a half within the British lines—not a defensible proposition.

To make some sense of Clinton's total mileage computation, Lamb shifted the high water mark of the British Light Infantry pursuit two and a half miles north of its undisputed starting point to the ravine at West 158th Street, east of Riverside Drive—her private "Hollow Way."

The British officer cited by Lamb was Captain George Harris of the 5th Regiment, who wrote an account of the battle to his uncle:

The 16th of September we were ordered to stand to our arms at 11 A.M. and were instantly trotted about three miles (without a halt to draw breath) to support a battalion of light infantry which had imprudently advanced so far without support as to be in danger of being cut off.

Captain Harris's estimate of his three-mile trot to the north matches Clinton's estimate of the distance covered by the Americans going south. With this new source, Lamb sought to implement the Benedict theory that the Battle of Harlem Heights was actually fought, not on Morningside Heights, but on the lower slopes of Washington Heights (which area, through the customary ironies of history and neighborhood custom, had by 1880 come to be known locally as "Harlem Heights").

The stage was now set for a real squabble. In the May 1880 issue of the New-York Historical Society's *Magazine of American History*, its editor John Austin Stevens sharply attacked the Lamb/Benedict theory. In his review of Mrs. Lamb's *History of New York City*, Stevens offered the first appearance in print of all the source material on which the 1876 Committee had based its choice of the Morningside Heights site. Apologizing for the somewhat circumstantial nature of the evidence, Stevens nonetheless insisted that the Committee's choice was perfectly justified, and the Harris-Clinton distance estimates were nothing more than natural exaggerations. Stevens tentatively identified the cannonballs recently unearthed near Audubon Terrace as artifacts from early stages of the successful British assault on Fort Washington, two months to the day after the Battle of Harlem Heights.

Stevens then struck what he considered a devastating blow to the Lamb/Benedict interpretation: he cited Washington's order of the day for 16 September. That morning the commander in chief had first ordered out the scouting party that eventually precipitated the full-scale battle, and followed with instructions to Brigadier General Gold Selleck Silliman[9] and his Connecticut militia to throw up entrenchments along a line roughly paralleling present-day West 147th Street. Stevens continued by quoting from a Continental soldier's diary to the effect that all of Silliman's militiamen had been kept busy digging entrenchments throughout the day, despite the "heavy firing below us."

Stevens demonstrated that the day's action probably never even came near 147th Street, effectively exploding the 158th Street/Audubon Terrace theory. Mrs. Lamb saw little light at the end of this tunnel. Although she never publicly recanted her published position, she demonstrated no further interest in the controversy.

But the second battle of Harlem Heights was far from over. In January 1881, undoubtedly as a tribute to the recently deceased Chancellor Benedict, his nephew carried on in fighting spirit by publishing the booklet earlier referred to, containing his uncle's original 1878 address. The nephew then took advantage of the opportunity to update the dispute by casting a few aspersions on Mr. Stevens's concept of definitive history.

To this the magazine editor, author of fifteen major articles and three books on the American Revolution, tartly replied in his April 1881 issue:

Of itself [the booklet] needs no notice or comment, the author having attained no reputation as an historian which gives weight

---

[9] Silliman soon left the army to serve as Attorney General of the State of Connecticut. He was later taken by the British as a civilian hostage and held for exchange.

to his individual opinion, when it conflicts with well-known facts, established by authority in accord with tradition. The subject would not receive further attention in this coloumn but for the prefix and appendix which accompany it. In both of these, Mr. Benedict [the nephew] charges this writer with unworthy personal motives in the review of Mrs. Lamb's work, and the condemnation of the new [battlefield] version which she adopted. And, secondly, with perverting facts and "garbling authorities and cooking maps," to use his own inelegant but characteristic words.[10]

No rejoinder from the nephew to this review of his and his uncle's booklet appeared in print, nor were any duels fought, and there the matter rested for another sixteen years unresolved; although Stevens had succeeded in demolishing the Audubon Terrace theory, he was unable to further substantiate the Morningside Heights version.

Then, in the fall of 1897, by moving uptown from its cramped quarters on Madison Avenue to the much heralded Revolutionary War battlefield, Columbia University became a generally interested party to the controversy. That year the Columbia University Press brought out what is still the most thoroughly researched work on the battle. Its author was Henry P. Johnston, a history professor at the College of the City of New York.

Johnston had long been interested in the controversy surrounding the proper identification of the battle site. In his 234-page *The Battle of Harlem Heights*, replete with maps and photographs, Johnston supported the majority view that the 16 September engagement took place on Morningside Heights; but he relocated the center of the battlefield farther west on the line of West 117th Street, closer to Broadway than to Morningside Drive. He justified this geographic shift on logical grounds, supported by his own photographs of a few remaining landmarks. His primary evidence was the location of historic Bloomingdale Road, the only through route over Morningside Heights in 1776; the others were farmhouse lanes. It was up and down Bloomingdale Road that much of this battle of advance and retreat, also involving some British artillery pieces, must have centered.[11]

[10] *Magazine of American History*, vol. VI, no. 7.

Johnston also argued that Knowlton's circling flank attack would
never have attempted to scale the sheer rock cliff of Morningside
Park. Instead, the author asserted, Knowlton's partially masked
column actually ascended the northern part of the Park's spine, a
rocky ridge (long since blasted away for the basements of a dozen
Morningside Drive apartment buildings). Johnston also disclosed for
the first time that the 1876 Committee had discarded yet another
candidate for the battlefield site, for in 1851, Benson J. Lossing's
two-volume *Pictorial Field-Book of the Revolution* had arbitrarily
placed the 16 September action on the flats, or "Plains," of Harlem,
above McGowan's Pass (near the north edge of present-day Central
Park). Following publication of Lossing's trailblazing but frequently
inaccurate work, the Battle of Harlem Heights was often referred to
as the "Battle of Harlem Plains!"

The Lamb/Benedict theory now seemed dead and buried, but
Johnston tried to stake it in its grave:

> Their version represents that four hundred light infantrymen,
> chasing Knowlton's Rangers, actually penetrated the American
> lines for more than a mile without being observed by other troops;
> that they blew their defiant bugle notes[12] in the rear of our main
> encampment; that Washington found it necessary to order out a
> flanking party to hem them in when there were ten American
> brigades already below them. In a word, we are given to understand
> that a mere detachment of the British army pushed through Wash-
> ington's lines, fought, at times, within four short blocks of his
> headquarters, made the circuit of his strong position, and then
> returned to Morningside Heights, carrying all their guns and
> wounded with them, and losing but 14 men killed. A proud day
> that, for the enemy!

Noting Washington's order of the day to Brigadier General
Silliman on digging entrenchments, Johnston concludes: ". . .[T]hey
present us with the singular spectacle of an army fortifying itself

---

[11] Below 118th Street, Bloomingdale Road ran slightly to the west of present day
Broadway, across the present Barnard College campus.

[12] The "gone to earth" horn call of the fox chase, contemptuously sounded by the
light infantry bugler and represented in some accounts of the battle as having irked
Washington into his initial maneuver.

against an enemy. . .engaged in "bloody battle" immediately in its rear."

A member of the American burial party on the evening of 16 September had written that "the British had already removed their own dead when we arrived." This, Johnston pointed out, would have required a double British crossing of the American lines. Feeling that he had satisfactorily disposed of the Lamb/Benedict theory for all time, Johnston ended his discussion. But he, too, had failed to supply any new evidence that could indisputably place the battlefield on Morningside Heights.

This time it took almost a decade for the argument to reignite. In the fall 1906 issue of the (retitled) *Magazine of History*, an article[13] appeared over the signature of Thomas Addis Emmet, M.D., a collector of historical manuscripts. Emmet rejected Johnston's careful and logical documentation. Basing most of his assertions as to geographical location on boyhood reminiscences, Emmet endeavored to prove that the battle was actually fought north—not south—of 125th Street. In passing, he could not resist a swipe at the new tenant on Morningside Heights, Columbia University:

> . . .[B]eyond the fact that the present site of Columbia University must necessarily be nearer the locality where the battle was fought, it has no greater claim, I believe, to that honor than has Union Square. . .I simply wish to offer a protest, in consequence of my knowledge that the history of our country is being constantly perverted and misstated.

Such dutifully published sentiments ignited a new firestorm among those members of the New-York Historical Society, who naively may have assumed that the controversy over the Morningside Heights battle site was settled.

In a blistering rejoinder[14] to Dr. Emmet in their January 1907 issue, the two new editors of the *Magazine of History*, Reginald Pelham Bolton and Edward Hagaman Hall, both well qualified and prolific local historians, took it for granted that Dr. Emmet was attempting to resurrect the discredited Lamb/Benedict Audubon Terrace theory. Bolton and Hall proceeded to skewer Emmet with

[13] "The Battle of Harlem Heights," *Magazine of History*, vol. IV, no. 3.

[14] "The Battle of Harlem Heights Again," *Magazine of History*, vol. V, no. 1.

all the by now traditional arguments, to which the instigator of the
uproar could only weakly reply that he, too, disbelieved the
Lamb/Benedict theory, and that:

> The battle was, in my judgment fought below the site of the present
> Convent of the Sacred Heart at the Point of Rocks, and along the
> irregular line of high ground, to the north of the plain to the east
> of Manhattanville."[15]

All these somewhat anticlimactic fireworks were fortunate in one
respect. New research by Bolton and Hall uncovered an entry from
Frank Moore's 1859 *Diary of the Revolution* that cleared up an old
problem by demonstrating the inaccuracy of the milestone numbers
on the Hobart sketch map. It also suggested that the mileage estimates
made by Captain Harris and General Clinton were indeed exaggerations. Moore's excerpt from a Revolutionary soldier's diary said
simply:

> 16 Sept. 1776
>     Our army is now between the nine and ten milestones, where
> they are strongly fortified and intrenched. The enemy's lines are
> about one mile and a half below them.

Contemporary maps showed the tenth milestone on the road to
King's Bridge to be near present-day 153rd Street, and the ninth stone
at 133rd Street. A mile and a half below the ninth stone would be
103rd Street, which supported the location of a British picket line at
108th Street. This circumstantial evidence seemed unassailable.

BUT WHERE was the Battle of Harlem Heights really fought? From
1907 through the middle of this century, the controversy rested. No
new evidence was introduced, no further shots were fired by either
side. In 1926, to properly celebrate the Revolutionary Sesquicenten-
nial, the Sons of the Revolution of the State of New York unveiled
a bronze bas-relief they had embedded in the wall of Columbia
University's School of Engineering, at 117th Street and Broadway.
Honoring the preferred battlefield site, the plaque depicted Colonel
Knowlton poised atop a rock just before taking the British musket

[15] A small village that later grew up in the Hollow Way.

ball in his breast, waving on his Rangers with an upraised sword. The historic plaque has ever since added considerable luster to Columbia's Revolutionary heritage.

MY OWN growing interest and involvement in this long-argued chain of events began in the 1940s, when, as an undergraduate at Columbia College, I first spotted that plaque. Since 1776, vast changes have altered the character of the Morningside Heights area as a great city grew up around it. As a geology student in Professor Armin Lobeck's cartography seminar, I eagerly undertook the preparation of an oversized color-keyed map[16] depicting the Harlem Heights battlefield site—then and now. It was while researching contemporary information for the 1776 base map in the stacks of Butler Library that I serendipitously encountered a previously unconnected piece of historic evidence. Thumbing through shelf after shelf of Revolutionary War material, I came across a book of map reproductions from the Sir Henry Clinton Papers at the Clements Library of the University of Michigan. My eye scanned the descriptive inventory and settled on "Map No. 143."

It was a military sketch map of Manhattan Island and its environs, prepared in the winter of 1776-77 by the ill-fated Major John André, then a junior officer with His Majesty's Royal Engineers. It may well have been André's cartographic skills that marked him for Sir Henry Clinton's initial attentions.

"Map No. 143" is an excellent example of André's ability to represent military locations. Four years later this ability would lead to his downfall and death on a Rockland County gibbet. On "Map No. 143" were a number of what André considered important points on Manhattan Island, their location keyed by large and decorative capital letters. One was simply labeled: "G Noltens Battle Sept. 16."

It was a notation that, until then, had gone completely unnoticed. Now it seemed to leap off the page. It was the future spy's rendering of "Knowlton"—the Ranger colonel who died at the head of his flanking column.

So a map did indeed exist, one that could identify the location of the "lost" battlefield, one for which Stevens and Johnston and Bolton and Hall would have moved mountains. All that time it had lain

---

[16] Now in the University's Columbiana Collection.

quietly undiscovered, along with the rest of the Clinton Papers, in the bottom of an old Clinton family trunk. Nothing here as world-shaking as unearthing a long-forgotten Shakespeare elegy, but in its own way, sufficient unto the day thereof.

In one sense it was too late. The last shot in the historians' second Battle of Harlem Heights had been fired half a century before. But at last the seventy-five-year-old controversy could be resolved. An investigation at the Clements Library showed the André map to be of sufficient scale to locate the battle site beyond any further doubt. A careful tracing of the original André map at the University of Michigan, superimposed on a current Geological Survey map of Manhattan Island reduced to identical scale, placed André's keying letter "G" precisely over Morningside Heights and Columbia University. And directly north of André's letter "G," a wavy double line clearly defined the Hollow Way.

Columbia University, described in its school song as "set upon a height," does indeed rest on a rocky plateau once splashed with the blood of young men fighting to assert their right to life, liberty, and the pursuit of happiness.

The pursuit of infighting is best left to historians.

# CHAPTER V

# A Shot in the Arm for Private Brown: Boston

*IN WHICH we experience the first half-year in the military life of a young Massachusetts soldier at the siege of Boston.*

*AMONG THE* forty American soldiers wounded in the Battle of Harlem Heights was twenty-three-year-old Private Obadiah Brown[1] from Gageborough, Massachusetts. Obadiah, the son of John and Lucy Underwood Brown, was born 9 August 1753, at Canterbury, Connecticut, thirty-five miles southeast of Hartford. His father was a farmer of reasonably distinguished ancestry, related to the Waldo and Adams families. While still a teenager, with his obligatory militia service behind him, Obadiah emigrated with his family from Canterbury more than 100 miles across the Connecticut border, into a newly settled (1771) corner of northwestern Massachusetts. This area in the foothills of the Berkshire Mountains, known as "Massachusetts Plantation Number 4," contained the tiny hamlet of Gageborough (now Windsor, Massachusetts), only twenty miles by crow flight from the long-established community of Native Americans living at Stockbridge and a dozen miles northeast of Pittsfield.

At the beginning of the Revolution, Obadiah was in no great hurry to enlist. For eight months after Lexington and Concord, he remained at home in Gageborough, wondering whether to join with the hundreds of other young Massachusetts militiamen helping to

---

[1] Not the identically-named Rhode Island manufacturer and educational philanthropist (1771-1822).

man the American siege lines around Boston. When he finally did decide to enlist, he made another decision as well. It was, insofar as posterity is concerned, most significant.

Though a relatively unschooled, laconic young farmer from the hills of western Massachusetts, Obadiah decided to bear written witness to the important military events that soon would be swirling about him. He began to keep a daily journal.

At first his guileless notations gave little hint of weighty matters. Obadiah followed his recording of the exhumation of Joseph Warren's mutilated corpse with the euphoric observation, on a sunny April morning: "I saw some barn swallows, which pleased my fancy."

But this was a terrifying war. Within a few months Obadiah was casually reporting: "One man killed with a shot that took his head off."

Obadiah was an assiduous diarist. During the entire year that he kept his journal, he never missed a day. He even scrawled an entry after he was wounded.

OBADIAH'S JOURNAL—now part of the collections of the Westchester County Historical Society is rectangular, and consists of sixty-four neatly trimmed rag-paper pages, 13-3/8" deep by 4-1/4" wide. Carefully prepared for the rigors of military life, the folded pages are sewn together with linen thread and bound in brown cowhide, suede side out. Physically, this diary of a young man's year of service at the start of the Revolution has weathered well. Its paper is still crisp, its ink entries still dark and shiny.

The events Obadiah inscribes are often tedious, only occasionally momentous. He writes about military life, his painful wounding, his slow and tortuous recovery. No warrior-philosopher, Obadiah was a patient shorthand reporter of the 1776 military scene at Boston and New York. We find occasional mention of letters to and from home (Gageborough was never more than 150 miles away); of a handful of letters to Lucy, the girl he left behind; and some words about Obadiah's comrades-in-arms. The reader finds considerable tension in his understated view of the Revolution "from the bottom up." Throughout the year, the accuracy of the camp rumors Obadiah dutifully reports shows him to be a discriminating listener.

Obadiah's penmanship is atrocious; his abbreviated, truncated spellings are worse. Consider his heroic grappling with that strange new army word, "fatigue": "Furteag"; "furtege"; "furteague"; "f'teague"; "forteag"; "feteague"; "firteague"; and "fateague." He finally settles on "furteague."

But this in no way diminishes Obadiah's stature as a genuine early American hero; even his general, Israel Putnam, was deficient in spelling and grammar, and in need of a military secretary at all times.

For easier comprehension, we take the liberty of correcting a few of Obadiah's misfires in the following transcript, particilarly in converting his abbreviations into more recognizable form. Explanatory material is [so bracketed].

*THE JOURNAL BEGINS* with a straightforward title page in capital letters:

OBADIAH BROWN
HIS BOOK
AND JOURNAL OF THE YEAR
OF OUR LORD 1776

BUNKER HILL
APRIL 22, 1776

Despite that late spring date, Obadiah actually began keeping some form of diary three months earlier, on the wintry day he left home, 30 January 1776. We can surmise that he transferred the initial entries from some less permanent record into this more substantial journal. Private Brown, encamped across the Charles River from Boston, probably acquired his new diary soon after the British evacuated the city, 17 March 1776.

He begins by recounting his trip across Massachusetts to Boston:

January 30 [Tuesday]: I set out from Gageborough to join the Army, and came down to [North]Hampton [thirty miles]. Stayed all night.

The winters during the years of the Revolution were among the hardest on record. Nonetheless, Obadiah's five-day, 128-mile journey afoot along the snowy roads of southern Massachusetts went quickly.

He makes no mention of traveling companions, and averages almost twenty-six miles a day—hard walking indeed.

> 31: Came to Colonel Howe's at Belcher[town] [fourteen miles]. Stayed all night.
> February 1: Came down to Lester [Leicester] [thirty-one miles]. Stayed all night.
> 2: Came to Sutbury [Sudbury] [twenty-seven miles]. Stayed all night.
> 3: Arrived at Cambridge [twenty-six miles].

Thus Obadiah reached his destination, the Revolutionary army encampment around Cambridge. Here he was only a cannon shot away from the 6,500 vastly outnumbered British troops manning Boston's defenses.

Obadiah's arrival in Cambridge on Saturday was timely. Even with a war on, early New England sabbatarians generally frowned on Lord's Day travel. John Jay, traveling in western Connecticut on official New York State business, thought it wise to request a Sunday laissez-passer from Governor Jonathan Trumbull.

Obadiah arrived at Cambridge headquarters seven months to the day after George Washington assumed command of the American Army and responsibility for converting 14,500 raucous raw recruits, mostly from New England, into a disciplined and effective fighting force.

> 4 [Sunday]: Went to the hospital, and saw 80 sick.

Obadiah was assigned to hospital duty, and billeted accordingly. Of the estimated 25,000 American soldiers who died in the Revolution, 8,500 perished while prisoners of war and 10,000 (39%) died of sickness in camp. The remaining 6,500 died in battle.

> 5: Our people killed two Regulars.

"Regular" was the colonial name for a soldier in the British Regular Army. For Obadiah, death—or the rumor of death—on the lines was still a noteworthy experience.

> 6: I went on fatigue [duty] to Lechmere Point.

Fatigue is military duty other than instruction or drill. Lechmere Point (now part of East Cambridge) was a strategic grassy peninsula (an island at high tide) southwest of Charlestown Neck dominating the Boston Harbor approaches to Cambridge. It had been the scene of several skirmishes with enemy foragers the previous year, and was now fortified by American fatigue parties, probably to keep otherwise idle soldiers busy and out of trouble—always a major problem in an army.

7: Two soldiers drank 33 glasses of brandy, and died.
8: I went to the store to fetch peas on my back.
9: I went on guard duty at Lechmere Point.
10: Two women were drummed out of camp.

Three days before relinquishing his Cambridge command to George Washington, Massachusetts General Artemas Ward frankly acknowledged the susceptibility to temptation of his relatively inactive men and ordered that "all possible care be taken that no lewd women come into camp" and that prostitutes already there be "brought to condign punishment." Eight months later, the problem persisted.

11 [Sunday]: A man in Cambridge very suddenly died.
12: I was on Quartermaster guard duty. One man was whipped 39 lashes.

Flogging was not an uncommon form of punishment in the Continental Army and remained a practice in both the military and navy into the 19th century.

13: I went to [Harvard] College to see Josiah Cleveland, but did not find him.

The Cleveland family, including Josiah and Jabez, referred to below, had been neighbors of the Browns in Canterbury.

14: 600 Regulars came out on Dorchester Hill burnt six houses and took one man and two boys. One of our men whipped.

This British reconnaissance in force surprised an American guard post facing enemy lines across Dorchester Neck.

15: I was on picket guard, and lay on my arms all night.
16: Orders came for one shilling [about two days' pay] to be taken out of a soldier's wages for every cartridge lost.
17: Orders for the militia to have powder horns instead of cartridge boxes.

Only a handful of American mills made gunpowder in 1775. The inadequate supply was critical in the earliest months of the Revolution, until surreptitiously furnished French gunpowder solved the shortage.

18 [Sunday]: I went to Meeting. Heard Mr. Swetting preach.
19: I was on picket guard.
20: I went to Lechmere Point on fatigue. The Regulars fired at us all day.
21: I went to town [Cambridge]. Saw John White.
22: I went to the hospital. It rained.
23: I was on guard duty at Lechmere Point.
24: I went on Lechmere guard duty.
25 [Sunday]: Seven Regulars deserted to Roxbury. The [British] ships fired at them with two 18-pounders, that carried to Lechmere Point.

The village of Roxbury anchored the American siege lines two miles south of Boston Neck; Lechmere was on the other side of the harbor. The enemy soldiers had been cooped up in Boston for almost a year. A British private's pay was eighty pence a day, with the bulk of that going back into his colonel's pocket "for expenses." For some, military duty (and patience) was wearing thin.

26: I was on picket guard. We heard the Regulars were going off.
27: I was on fatigue [duty]. One steeple pulled down.

The British were methodically eliminating any possible covert signal towers.

28: I was off duty.
29: I was on guard duty; I stood ten hours sentry duty.

March 1: I was at home. Mr. Goodrich was sick.
2: I was at home.
3 [Sunday]: I was on picket guard. Bombs flew thick.
4: Went on Lechmere guard duty. Stood sentry where the balls and shells flew like hailstones. Three bombs fell in the fort. One Indian was killed. Our people built two forts on Dorchester Hill.

The dead Native American soldier at the Lechmere fort was probably from Stockbridge. Obadiah's last sentence, one of the weightiest in the journal, concerns a checkmate in the lengthy American siege of Boston. Within two weeks of the date of the entry, the British would be forced to withdraw to Nova Scotia. The long awaited heavy artillery, stripped by General Henry Knox's teamsters from the ramparts of New York's Fort Ticonderoga and laboriously sledged hundreds of miles through winter snows, finally arrived in Cambridge. Protected by barrels of sand and "chandeliers" (wicker baskets filled with chunks of frozen earth), the mortars and heavy cannon were emplaced overnight on Dorchester Heights, commanding Boston town and harbor, by General John Thomas and 2,000 men. "The rebels have done more in one night than my whole army could do in months," British commander Sir William Howe ruefully remarked. An attempt by the British the following day to capture the American position was washed out by an early spring rainstorm. British military ardor was equally wetted down, perhaps by memories of their catastrophic frontal attack on Bunker Hill. Four days later, the enemy requested permission from the Americans to quietly depart Boston by sea. They had solved Washington's (and Congress's) greatest dilemma—how to rid Boston of its occupiers without destroying the city in the process.

5: I went to the hospital to take care of Mr. Goodrich. There was an alarm.
6: Our people filled 500 hogsheads with sand to kill the Regulars. One man, found dead in the [enemy] fire, supposed to be murdered.
7: Captain Spaulding's Negro died.

Like British army officers with their personal orderlies (or batmen), many Continental officers from both northern and southern states brought manservants, usually household slaves, onto the field. General Washington was accompanied by his African-American butler. Also enshrined in our Revolutionary iconography is Peter Salem, a slave belonging to Lieutenant Thomas Grosvenor of the 3rd Connecticut Regiment (see *Chapter VIII*).

> 8: One man died here. Fifty men went to Bunker Hill as spies [lookouts]. A flag or truce came out of Boston to our people, to have three days and they would go off in peace.
> 9: There came orders to fire at Boston. The firing began at night. Four men killed at Dorchester Point.

Distrusting the enemy negotiators, the Americans continued to fortify Dorchester Heights. The British kept up a cannonade of the soldiers at work on Nook's Hill.

> 10 [Sunday]: Twenty-five sail went out of Boston. The Regulars seemed in a great confusion.

All the while, almost as if to use up cannonballs and powder, the relatively ineffective enemy bombardment continued.

> 11: Two men died here. Mr. Jabez Cleveland was one of them. One man drummed out of the camp.
> 12: One regiment of men went to Roxbury from Cambridge. We saw the flashes of cannon off at sea at night.

Offshore, Captain John Manley's thirty-two-gun USS *Hancock*, accompanied by consorts, had been cruising the sea lanes near Boston, picking off smaller British warships and merchantmen.

> 13: I went down to the barracks, and returned home again.
> 14: A man died in the room where I was.
> 15: One regiment of riflemen, with some young women from Cambridge, marched for New York [City]. Two Regulars deserted from Boston. Fifteen [naval] prisoners that [Captain John] Manley took came to Cambridge. Colonel [John] Paterson's barracks were burnt.

With the British evacuation of Boston, Washington surmised that the next enemy objective would be New York City, 200 miles away. He already had agreed to Congress's request to detach General

Charles Lee to stiffen New York's defenses and now began to redeploy his army.

There was never any serious prohibition of reasonable numbers of women following the troops. For every doxy Obadiah watched being ceremoniously drummed out of Cambridge camp, tens of sober and industrious females were allowed to remain behind unmolested to minister to everyday (and night) needs.

Colonel (later General) John Paterson commanded a militia regiment raised in the Berkshires before the beginning of the Revolution. The Stockbridge Native Americans initially served in his command, as did Deborah Sampson (see *Chapter VII*).

> 16: I had a bad cold, etc.
> 17 [Sunday]: Lord Howe and his crew left Boston and Bunker Hill. Went down between our people, who took possession of them both. They wrote on their barracks, "Brother Jonathan, you're welcome to Bunker Hill."

March 17th, the first of more than two centuries of Boston "Evacuation Day" celebrations, was a day of rejoicing for all Americans (tempered only by continuous bad news from the faltering invasion of Canada). During the nine months following the battle on 17 June 1775, the enemy had maintained barrack installations on the Bunker/Breed's Hill peninsula.

> 18: One man died in the hospital. Four regiments marched for New York.
> 19: One man died here. The Regulars blew up Castle [William]. One of our officers killed a Tory's Negro. One of our men whipped 30 lashes.

Castle William stood on Castle Island near the Dorchester peninsula. It was the last stronghold retained by the British to guard the inner channel to Boston Harbor. It was abandoned and blown up by the enemy's 64th Regiment on the night of the 18th.

> 20: Three regiments of men went into Boston.
> 21: I was somewhat not well.
> 22: Our Regiment went into Boston.
> 23: I saw a rifleman 20 years old, six feet seven inches high.

24 [Sunday]: I went down to our barracks, and back again.
25: Twenty-five sail of ships went off. One hundred horses were
sold at vendue [auction], taken from the Regulars.
26: Some cannon fired from the ships.
27: One man died here. I went on Bunker Hill, and into Boston.
Saw four men whipped. Thirty-five sail of ships went off. Stayed
all night.

Grudgingly abandoning their Boston toehold, 120 British warships, transports, and other craft, crammed with thousands of fleeing
loyalists, anchored for more than a week in Nantasket Roads, five
miles below the port city. Of this maneuver Washington remarked:
"The enemy has the best knack at puzzling people I ever met with."
Lord Howe's evacuation fleet eventually set its secret course for
Halifax, 400 miles away, to spend three months in refitting and
regrouping. Not all the warships sailed with Howe; a number remained behind in Nantasket Roads to harrass the area with minor
actions and shore attacks.

28: Went to the hospital.
29: One man died here. Several regiments from Cambridge
marched for New York.
30: I helped bury a man.
31 [Sunday]: I heard our Regiment is going to New York.
April 1: The militia was discharged. Three regiments of men
marched to Rhode Island; we heard 30 ships of Regulars landed
there.

The American Army continued its massive redeployment. The
rumor of a British landing on the shores of Narragansett Bay proved
to be only the first of a long series of false alarms. The actual
whereabouts of Lord Howe's invasion fleet remained a subject of
great speculation until the arrival, from Halifax, of its initial units off
New York Harbor (Sandy Hook NJ) on 27 June.

2: Old Coffin struck a fellow, and I pulled him off.
3: I taped my shoes; it was a rainy day.
4: I went to Cobble Hill, Bunker Hill, and Prospect Hill, and
returned home to the hospital; I was tired enough. One man died
here.
5: One man died here. I went to Cambridge and back again.

6: A very warm day. I went to Cambridge.

7 [Sunday]: One man had his leg cut all to bits; one good stout piece cut out.

8: The body of General [Joseph] Warren was carried from Bunker Hill to Boston, and buried. One man died here.

Militia General Joseph Warren, brilliant Boston physician and Revolutionary orator of great political promise, had met his death nine months earlier, shot in the head in the final hand-to-hand combat at Bunker Hill. It was a bloody engagement that cost the British dearly—one quarter of their North American officer corps in a single afternoon. Warren's body, thrown by the enemy into a common grave, was exhumed and identified by a pair of false teeth made for him by his friend and fellow activist Paul Revere. Warren's remains, carried to the Old Granary Burying Ground, would be moved twice more—in 1825, to an honorary vault in St. Paul's Chapel, and in 1855, to his final resting place in Forest Hills Cemetery in Jamaica Plain.

9: I saw some barn swallows, which pleased my fancy.

10: We heard Quebec was taken [by the British] and that we lost 800 men. I went to Bunker Hill and back. One rifleman died here.

Obadiah referred not only to the American expeditionary force's New Year's eve defeat at the gates of Quebec City, for "Quebec" was the general term for much of eastern Canada, including the city of Montreal. On 17 January, Washington had learned of the calamitous death of General Richard Montgomery (and the wounding of Benedict Arnold) in the assault on Quebec City.

11: One man died here.

12: A young man named Thomas Pierce had his leg cut off close to his knee, which was done by a man pushing him down over a chest.

By now, Obadiah had observed several major operations and the deaths of seventeen men at the camp hospital.

13: I washed five shirts and three pairs of stockings.

14 [Sunday]: S.D. I was at home in the hospital.

15: I went to Cambridge and back, and then to Bunker Hill, and to Boston's fortification gate, and all the forts, and home again.
16: I was at home, and watched with a man who had his leg cut off.
17: I went to Cambridge, and back again.
18: The man died who had his leg cut off, with the quick consumption. He died much resigned to the will of God.
19: I helped bury that man.
20: Four Tories went by here, going to Worcester. One man died in the hospital.
21 [Sunday]: S.D. I went to Bunker Hill and joined my Company.
22: I went into Boston and back.
23: I went on fatigue. One man deserted out of our Company.

With the bulk of the army now in New York City—Washington himself had arrived on 13 April—it became increasingly necessary to make work for the small group of soldiers left behind in Cambridge.

24: I was on fatigue at Charlestown Point.
25: I went into Boston in the morning after bread. Came back. Went on fatigue, etc., which is hard.
26: I went to the hospital, and came back. Went on guard duty; six prisoners in the guard house.
27: I went to Boston and back. Saw John Stevens. Heard Lieutenant Lionw'n and Perris Sprague are dead.
28 [Sunday]: S.D. I wasn't well.
29: Five men whipped twenty lashes apiece for deserting. I went on fatigue.
30: Rained all day; almost no fatigue.
May 1: I was on fatigue. One man whipped 20 lashes. It was a cold wintry day.
2: I was on fatigue.
3: I went into Boston and back again, and went on fatigue.
4: I went on Noddle Island on fatigue. One ship sailed out.

Exactly one year earlier, Noddle's Island, a strategic point on the northeastern shore of Boston Harbor, had been the scene of a deadly skirmish between Royal Marines and American militia under General Putnam.

5 [Sunday]: S.D. I was on guard duty at the blockhouse.
6: One man drowned in Boston. Robert Walker and Elijah Clark came to see me; I was at home. I sent a letter home.

7: I went on Noddle's Island fatigue. We heard our people took two brigs from the Regulars today.
8: I went on fatigue. Went into Boston twice. It rained.
9: I went on Noddle's Island fatigue.
10: I was on fatigue again, and I wish it was done.
11: I went on Noddle's Island fatigue again.
12 [Sunday]: I was on fatigue on Charlestown Point, drawing cannon, and carrying houses on my back.
13: I was on guard duty.
14: I went into Boston. One of our privateers took a transport from the Regulars, in sight of Boston. One of our ships went out after it.

USS *Hancock*, under its new captain, Samuel Tucker, was still patrolling Massachusetts Bay in hopes of picking up any stray merchantmen sailing from England in April, i.e., before hearing news of the fall of Boston. On 7 May off Salem, Tucker captured *Jane* and *William*, heavy laden with military supplies.

15: I was on fatigue.
16: I went into Boston. My hand was lame, so that I could not work.
17: Our privateers took on a ship of 475 tons, which had 75 tons of powder on board. It was Fast Day. Our people saw 60 sail of ships lying off in the Bay.

The fast probably celebrated the British evacuation of Boston two months earlier.

18: It was a rainy day; no fatigue.
19 [Sunday]: S.D. I was on guard duty. Received a letter from Father and one from Dwyar Reid. The cannon roared off at sea at night. Thirteen boats, with 20 Regulars in each, went to take the privateer that took the ship. They killed the captain and wounded two more. The Regular loss was thought to be great; 35 bodies washed upon the shore. They fought sword in hand. The Regulars left men and arms behind.

After taking a British transport from Cork, the schooner USS *Franklin* ran aground on a sandbar off Nantasket Roads's Point Shirley. On the night of 19 May, *Franklin* was attacked by a 200-man enemy naval force in small boats. James Mugford of Marblehead, the

American captain, was killed, and several members of his twenty-one-man crew were wounded. After a half-hour struggle, the British boarding party was repulsed and the ship was refloated.

20: I went into Boston to see the ship that was taken.
21: I went on fatigue. As I went to go out of the fort, a sentry fired at me. We heard our people were defeated at Quebec. I sent a letter home.

Like many other soldiers before and since, Obadiah narrowly escaped "friendly fire."

22: I went on fatigue, etc.
23: I was on fatigue, carrying apple tree limbs on my back.
24: I was on guard duty; the countersign was "sharp."
25: I was off duty.
26 [Sunday]: S.D. One Negro whipped. I was on fatigue.
27: I was on fatigue, etc.
28: I was on guard duty.
29: Election Day. I went into Boston twice, and heard the chime of bells.
30: I went into Boston after bread and vinegar, etc., three times.
31: I went on fatigue, which was nothing new.
June 1: I went on guard duty at Mystic powder house.

This was the storage facilty above Winter Hill that Benjamin Thompson secretly reconnoitered and described to General Howe in the fall of 1775.

2 [Sunday]: S.D. It rained some. I went on guard duty at the powder house.
3: I was on guard duty. No news to write.
4: A team carried off 205 barrels of powder from the powder house.
5: I wrote two letters; one for Lucy, and one for John. I had two hours to stand sentry out of 20, which was easy.
6: I went down to Bunker Hill, and back again. The countersign was "Yankee."
7: Went down to Bunker Hill to guard a prisoner. Met Uncle Fisk. Sent two letters home, and returned back.
8: I was released from powder house guard duty. Came to Bunker Hill. Wrote a letter to Father; sent it by Samuel Breeder.

9 [Sunday]: S.D. I was at home. Saw the ships plying around. Our privateers were around, chasing a ship. The cannon roared.

Captain William Burke's USS *Warren*, Captain Daniel Waters's *Lee*, and Captain John Ayres's *Lynch*, captured the British transport HMS *Anne*.

10: I was on fatigue in the forenoon. In the afternoon I went to Boston and bought one silk handkerchief.
11: I was on fatigue. A flag of truce went in the Commodore's ship, and was used well, they said. Our people fought well, more like devils than men.
12: Fatigue again.
13: Orders came for our people to go down to Long Island, to drive off the ships. We got there about ten o'clock at night. Carried on two 18-pounders, two nine-pounders, two field pieces, and one 13-inch mortar. Our regiment was for guard duty; the rest of the men went to work.

The seaward tip of Long Island at the southeast corner of Boston Harbor, below Dorchester, was within cannon range of a still active British naval anchorage. Obadiah here records the surreptitious nighttime loading of seven pieces of Ticonderoga artillery from Dorchester to surprise and drive off the twelve enemy warships.

14: Soon as daylight appeared, the ships lay all in sight; seven ships, two brigs, and three schooners. With the sun half an hour high, we began to fire shots and shells; it made the ships tremble. Cut the admiral's yardarm so it hung down, shot through. The admiral fired at us, but could not reach us. They weighed their anchors, and pushed off. None of our people were hurt by them. They blew up the lighthouse. We came home. The cannon and muskets roared well.

This engagement between a British squadron, led by the fifty-gun HMS *Renown* and American onshore artillery, was Obadiah's baptism by fire. His excitement is evident; this is his longest diary entry to date. The previous July, heavy skirmishing had raged around the Boston harbor lighthouse on Great Brewster Island, a mile off Nantasket Point. The lighthouse was set afire by an American party

under Major Joseph Vose, but it was soon restored by the British—
who now destroyed it entirely.

> 15: I was at home. Received a letter from Uncle E. Brown. Went
> to Boston, and returned home again.
> 16 [Sunday]: I sent one letter to Uncle Pellet, and one to Waldo
> [his brother] by Jonathan Downing. I wrote one for Father, and
> one for Colonel Sprague, and one for Dwyar Reid, and one for
> Uncle E. Brown. Sunday, etc. Our people took one ship and one
> brig, and 220 prisoners.

With the brisk and successful action of 13-14 June, Obadiah had
something to write home about. That day, USS *Franklin*, USS *Lee*,
USS *Lynch*, USS *Warren*, and USS *Defence* together attacked and
captured HMS *Annabella* and HMS *George* in Massachusetts Bay. Of
the enemy, twelve were killed and thirteen wounded in the action;
nine Americans were wounded.

> 17: I was on fatigue.
> 18: I was on fatigue. Sent a letter to Uncle E. Brown, by Captain
> Cleveland. Our privateers took a ship with 110 Regulars on board.

Off Marblehead, Captain John Fisk and USS *Tyrannicide* had
captured HMS *Lord Howe*. For the next few weeks, until the main
enemy invasion base shifted to New York City, attacks on British
ships straggling toward Boston continued.

> 19: I went on fatigue. Our people took another ship.
> 20: I was on guard duty. We took another ship.
> 21: I sent a letter home to Father. Went on fatigue.
> 22: I was on fatigue. It was very warm weather, etc.
> 23 [Sunday]: S.Day. No duty. I saw ten ships in sight of Boston.
> Three hundred of our men went down to Long Island to work.
> 24: I went on forenoon fatigue. In the afternoon I laid walls. Went
> in swimming at night.
> 25: I was on guard duty. Very warm weather indeed. I went in
> swimming again.
> 26: Our Company drilled all day. Marched up to Mystic, and tired
> us very much.
> 27: No fatigue. I laid walls.

28:I mowed all day; had three shillings for my day's work. We heard our people were driven from Quebec to this side of the Lakes.

Bad news spreads swiftly, particularly in an army. On 14 June, driven by mounting enemy pressure, the remainder of General John Sullivan's smallpox-wracked expeditionary forces began their retreat from the Canadian border town of Sorel to the northern end of Lake Champlain.

29: I was on guard duty. It was very warm weather.
30 [Sunday]: S.Day. I went to Noddle's Island, and returned home.
July 1: I went to Boston and sent three letters home by E. Clark: one to Father, one to John, and one to Lucy, and returned home.
2: I went to Boston after a boat, to move down to the Castle [William]. We went down there with one boatload. It rained, and I returned back.
3: We went down with the other load, and went into tents.
4: I had a pain in my head, and felt not well. There were 300 soldiers innoculated in Boston, with a number of others.

The Continental Army's order against self-innoculation against smallpox was being ignored. Soldiers were deliberately infecting themselves with the attenuated pus of others recovering from the virus. In almost all cases, the results proved favorable.

5: We heard from New York that our people had a a battle there, and killed and took 7,000 Regulars, and lost 2,000, but kept their ground. It was a shower day, and wet our tents.

For once, the rumors of battle Obadiah recorded were premature. Although the British transports had begun to arrive in New York Harbor from Nova Scotia by the end of June, Sir William Howe was not prepared to move his 15,000 Regulars and Hessian mercenaries to Long Island (Brooklyn) to commence hostilities until 22 August.

6: The general's orders were that no one was to be innoculated after today. I was not well.
7 [Sunday]: S.Day. I was ordered on guard duty, but by reason of being not well, I did not go.

8: We heard that a Yankee sloop took two prizes the day before yesterday. One of them came to Boston today. I went on fatigue.
9: I was on fatigue. One prize ship came into Boston.
10: I was on fatigue. The other ship came in. There was the most terrible thunder shower that ever I saw. It blew our tents down and wet us all over.
11: I was freed from duty to shave the Company.
12: Our Company drilled all day. Two men whipped 39 lashes apiece, at night.
13: A sergeant died with the smallpox, belonging to Perry's Company.
14 [Sunday]: S.day. It rained, etc.
15: Orders came for our Regiment and one more to march for Ticonderoga.

As part of a grand British War Office strategy to split New England from the rest of what were, since 4 July, "free and independent States," the enemy was now threatening both ends of the long Hudson River Valley, from New York City to the south (under Sir William Howe) to Lake Champlain to the north (under Sir Guy Carleton). Most of the garrison left to defend Boston against surprise attack was now being reassigned; Obadiah's regiment was ordered to Fort Ticonderoga at the southern end of Lake Champlain.

But it was a moment of some indecision—

16: Orders came for us to march to New York.

—and the regiment instead began preparations for an overland march southwest through the countryside to New London, Connecticut. There it would take ship ninety-five sea miles, via relatively protected Long Island Sound, to the East River, "back door" to New York City.

17: We were fixing up to go our journey.
18: We set out for New York. Went to Dorchester and stayed all night.
19: We went through Roxbury and Jamaica Plain into Dedham [nine miles], and stayed all night.
20: Marched through Walpole and Wrentham into Attleburg [Attleboro] [eighteen miles]. Stayed all night.

21 [Sunday]: S.Day. Went through Rehoboth into Providence [Rhode Island] [sixteen miles]. Stayed all night.

The army continued marching on Sunday; observance of the sabbath gave way to military necessity

22: Went through Cranson [Cranston] and Cituate [North Scituate] into Coventry [Washington] [eight miles], and stayed all night.
23: Came through Volentown [Voluntown, Connecticut] and Plainfield and part of Canterbury into Newait [Newent] [thirty-one miles]. Stayed all night.
24: I went into Norwich [eight miles]; Uncle Pellet and Aunt were at Norwich, but I could not find them. At night we went from Norwich through Pomechogg [Poquetanuck] into New London [fourteen miles], which was seven miles in 40 minutes.

Obadiah was obviously proud of his regiment's covering 103 miles in six days, each soldier carrying full pack, cartridge box, and musket. He hails their last burst of marching speed into the outskirts of New London at ten and a half miles per hour, a figure that stretches the imagination.

25: Came into the town of New London.

Five years later, Benedict Arnold, rewarded with $100,000 and a major general's commission in the British Army, would lead a punitive expedition of 1,700 Regulars, German mercenaries, and tories up the Thames River to burn New London, his old home town, to the ground.

CHAPTER VI

# *A Shot in the Arm for Private Brown: New York*

*IN WHICH our soldier-diarist, sailing for New York City, continues his "bottom-up" observations of 1776 army life and is seriously wounded at Harlem Heights.*

> July 26: A young man hanged himself. We set sail for New York. Sailed to the lighthouse, and stayed all night.
> 27: We set sail again, but the wind failed and we dropped anchor until after noon. Then set out again, and went 60 or 70 miles by night.
> 28 [Sunday]: S.day. We came to the mouth of Hell Gate. Lay at anchor all night.

Hell Gate is the turbulent strait where the tides of Long Island Sound battle those of New York's East River.

> 29: We went through to [New] York, and lay at anchor until towards night; then returned to Hell Gate, and landed there.

Obadiah's regiment was held in reserve, pulling garrison duty in a small fortification (a "hornwork") on Horn Hook on upper Manhattan Island. This strategic point of land at 88th Street, opposite the northern tip of Blackwell's Island, commanded the East River passage.[1]

---

[1] Now the site of Gracie Mansion, official home of New York City's mayor.

The main American defensive force was divided between what then comprised the city of Manhattan ten miles south and Brooklyn Heights across the East River.

30: The Colonel's orders were that no soldier was to go more than eight rods [one-quarter mile] from the Fort.
31: I saw Gageborough men in York; six of them, and I was much pleased to hear of home.

Obadiah was beset by curiosity. Despite his colonel's order, he hiked the six miles south along the Post (Kingsbridge) Road to the city. The population of New York had swelled from 20,000 to 30,000 in the three months since Washington's arrival from Boston on 13 April. The dusty streets of New York were jammed with Continental soldiers, whom Washington affectionately referred to as his "ragged boys." Many of them had never seen a big city before.

Throughout the late spring and early summer, the American commander, with agonizingly slow attention to detail, strived to master the complex logistics of leading the relatively undisciplined revolutionary army. To an unusual degree, he called upon the strategic counsel of his general officers, each of whom had been carefully selected by Congress to represent a different region of the rebellion.

August 1: I sent a letter home to Father, and was not well. Forty-five men died in New York.
2: Our regiment drilled, etc.
3: The cannon roared very keen. Our people drove a ship up the river, when they tried to come down.

On 21 July, the war in the north moved up the Hudson River, temporarily bypassing New York City. Captain Hyde Parker's HMS *Phoenix* and Captain James Wallace's HMS *Rose* easily ran past the batteries at Forts Washington and Lee and sailed into the Tappan Zee, interdicting supply ships and harassing patriot farmers on either side of the river. On 3 August, four American row galleys, manned by Connecticut watermen, fired on the British warships (one had grounded), but failed to press home the attack, causing only minor damage.

4 [Sunday]: Sd. Orders came for every man to be whipped that
swore an oath; 39 lashes.
5: I was troubled with the camp disorder, but got better at night.

Sanitary conditions in the impromptu camps were deplorable;
the Continental Army often had as many ill and wounded soldiers
in the hospital as were fit for duty. Throughout August and September, Obadiah was plagued by the "camp disorder," endemic bacillary
dysentery and resultant weakness and diarrhea. Overcrowded living
and unsanitary food preparation led to contamination. One of Washington's first orders upon arrival called for the immediate digging of
"necessaries." Until then, many of his New York garrison had been
forced to relieve themselves in stables and alleyways.

6: Three men whipped for desertion.
7: A flag of truce came out from the Regulars, and we went to them.
We thought they would pick a battle soon.

Within the scope of his commission, General Howe did much to
avoid aggressive prosecution of the war, in which the odds were
certainly stacked in his favor. Even after winning the Battle of Long
Island, with his troops poised for their successful invasion of Manhattan, the British commander authorized a secret 11 September
"peace conference" on Staten Island, offering Congress's commissioner Benjamin Franklin what turned out to be unacceptable terms
for an immediate end to the hostilities.

8: Three men whipped; two for desertion, one for refusing to do
duty. I sent a letter to Father by the post. It was Fast Day; we had
two sermons preached. One text was Jeremiah 4-14, the other was
Exodus 3-4; fine sermons indeed.

Throughout the Revolution, pulpits strove to convince the Revolutionaries that God was indeed on their side. The text from Jeremiah
may have been chosen with an eye on the enemy's progress down
Lake Champlain from Canada: "...out of the north an evil shall break
forth upon all the inhabitants of the land." Exodus 3 is Moses and
the burning bush.

9: I was 23 years old, etc. No news remarkable to write.

10: Orders came for every man to have things in readiness for a moment's warning, and every man to have half a pint of rum for the expedition.
11 [Sunday]: S.Day. I went to the city of York, and got some things: two shirts and one pair of trousers. Had two letters from Father, and Lucy, and some good news in the letters. General Lee came to York with 1,500 men.

Congress had appointed English-born General Charles Lee of Virginia (who had served with Washington under Braddock) as second in command of the Continental Army. Early in 1776, Lee had been sent to New York from Boston, to prepare the city against attack. In March, Congress reassigned Lee to Virginia and the Carolinas, to reorganize American military activities there. This time, camp rumor led Obadiah astray: on 11 August, Lee was still en route back to New York from the successful American defense of Charleston, South Carolina.

12: The militia was sent for to come into York, in order for a battle. James Watkins died.
13: Some cannon fired up the North River,[2] supposed to be at the ships.
14: The troops came in very thick. Four thousand came by land, and a great number by sea.
15: The troops came in like showers of rain. It was warm weather.
16: I received a letter from Father, by Mr. Warren. A man died in our regiment. There were 15,000 men in York unfit for duty.

Obadiah vastly overestimated the problem of illness. Even with the new arrivals, there were only about 10,000 men in Washington's entire command.

17: No news strange to write:
18 [Sunday]: The ships got down the North River and got to the fleet. Our people fired at them, and shot them through and through. S.Day etc.

---

[2] The original appellation for Hudson's River, distinguishing it from the "South (Delaware) River."

HMS *Phoenix* and HMS *Rose* had been unsuccessfully attacked by a small flotilla of American fireships near Yonkers on the night of 16 August. It was a close call for the British ships (one tender was burned), and the enemy captains decided to rerun the guns of Forts Washington and Lee to rejoin their fleet in New York's Upper Bay. The British warships actually suffered little damage.

19: The troops came in as thick as hops. Sergeant Martin died, etc.

Most of these welcome reinforcements were enthusiastic but poorly organized Westchester County and Connecticut militia, who had the bad habit of fading away at the sound of cannon fire. The only troops Washington could reasonably rely on were the enlisted Continentals.

20: I was very poor with the camp disorder, and rheumatism, but drank brandy and loaf sugar plentifully, which helped me.
21: I was poor again. Had no stomach for my victuals. It was very hot. There came up a shower in the afternoon which held till late in the night, with the most terrible thunder and lightning that ever I saw. Seven men died in York.
22: News came that England was for making peace with America, and had sent letters to the Congress. The Regulars landed on Long Island.

Temporarily putting aside peaceful gestures, Howe decided that the best way into New York City was not by direct assault, but by a roundabout route via Long Island and Brooklyn. On 22 August, with the Royal Navy heavily bombarding the shoreline, he disembarked on Long Island most of his 17,000-man British and German expeditionary force and began to probe the American positions with cavalry patrols and infantry scouting parties. American troops under General John Sullivan encountered one such British advance unit near the village of Flatbush; two of his men were wounded.

23: The cannon roared on Long Island. The news was that our people had surrounded the Regulars. A man whipped 39 lashes.

Washington continued to ferry troops across the East River to strengthen his positions on Brooklyn Heights. Obadiah's regiment was still held in reserve at Horn Hook.

24: I went to the city. Heard the cannon roar, but could get no certain news. Mr. Warren died. I went to the hospital. Stayed all night.
25 [Sunday]: S.d. The cannon roared all day at Long Island, but got no news as to which side was like to conquer.
26: I took a portion of physic, which done me good. Our people took 30 or 40 prisoners. At night the Regulars drove our people a mile and a half.

Units of General Lord Stirling's brigade skirmished with a party of Hessians, killing several.

27: They had a bloody battle. Our people drove them back again. I think it is sober times. Reuben Simonds died and was buried, and two more died in the same room.

General Howe ferried the rest of his 17,000 British and German troops ashore on Long Island, and began the long awaited full-scale battle. Royal Navy broadsides, in a good show of interservice cooperation, took turns cannonading the beaches and foreshore. With adroit maneuvering and sheer strength of numbers, the enemy quickly overran or pushed back Washington's 10,000-man army. Howe inflicted 1,097 casualties and captured Generals Stirling and Sullivan. The patriots' position, with their backs to the East River, was bleak.

28: A number of riflemen ran away from Long Island, but were sent back. One man died in the hospital. The Regulars tried to force our line three times, but got drove back.
29: It was a rainy day. A number of our men went to the Island, in sight of the Regulars, and returned home. The news is that our people all left the Island, and brought away their cannon and baggage, which is likely true. At night we had certain news of the retreat.

For two days the victorious Howe had hardly moved a muscle, while Washington vacillated between reinforcement or withdrawal. Then, on 29 August, in one of the most dramatic maneuvers in the history of warfare, the "Old Fox," under cover of night and fog, rowed the entire American army back across the East River into Manhattan with all their artillery and most of their baggage. Incredibly, not a man was lost.

30: Lieutenant Cleveland went on the Island, and brought off a number of cows and horses. The Regulars came in sight, with their Light Horse and a number of Foot and Tories. Our people came off, and left a great number of cattle.

31: Our men went on Long Island, and brought off their cannon with a general leave. We were somewhat uneasy. Two Brigadiers came to join us.

September 1 [Sunday]: S.day. I went to Colonel Smith's Regiment to see my friends, etc.

2: The cannon roared some. One ship came up in sight of our Fort.

3: I never saw such times before. I said but little, but thought we needed more. Some cannon fired at the ship. We cut one barge in two. We had an alarm at night.

4: Shots and shells flew. We were under arms, etc. The ship went down the Sound again. The fire was warm between the enemy and our people.

5: The cannon blazed away from each party. I went into the Rangering service.

This brief mention marks Obadiah's fateful decision to volunteer for the Connecticut Rangers, bidding farewell to his comrades at Horn Hook. As we have seen, the Rangers were an elite infantry strike force, newly organized by thirty-six-year-old Lieutenant Colonel Thomas Knowlton of Connecticut, a distinguished veteran of Bunker Hill and the French and Indian Wars, including Albemarle's 1762 siege of Havana.

6: Some of the Rangers drove off the guard on Long Island, and took a number of guns and a spyglass worth $18. I was on guard duty.

7: The Regulars were in great preparation for battle.

Howe was preparing, with customary caution, a vigorous amphibious assault over a long stretch of the East River. It was already
being supported by a continous cannonade. Centered on Kip's Bay
(present-day 34th Street), the enemy attack was designed to roll up
the American left on lower Manhattan Island.

> 8 [Sunday]: S.Day. Very early in the morning, they opened three
> batteries. The shots and shells flew very thick. They shot one
> 18-pound ball through a man's breast. We moved up to Harlem.

Harlem was a farming community straddling the Post Road, en
route to strategic King's Bridge at the northern tip of Manhattan
Island.

> 9: The cannonading held very brisk. I received a letter from
> Nehemiah Cleveland. I was very sick at night.
> 10: The earth nearly trembled with the sound of cannon. The
> Regulars landed on another island near us. A boy took up a shell
> to get the powder out, and another boy struck on it, to get the fuse
> out. It went off, and tore one boy's thigh all to pieces. Alarm at
> night.

A British landing party drove the twenty-man American garrison
from Montresor's (now Randall's) Island, above Horn Hook in the
East River. Two enemy attackers were wounded.

> 11: The cannon played very brisk. No great news to be heard.
> 12: The Rose man-of-war came down the Sound, and hove to close
> by us. One man killed with a shot that took his head off; we looked
> out for breakers.

Captain Wallace's ubiquitous HMS *Rose* was returning from a
one-ship punitive raid/bombardment of Long Island Sound shore
towns. Obadiah, now with the Rangers, missed an unsuccessful
enemy attack on his old comrades at Horn Hook in which one British
soldier was killed and four wounded. On this day, too, one of
Obadiah's fellow Rangers, Captain Nathan Hale, volunteered to
make his way secretly behind British lines in New York City to
determine enemy troop strength and disposition.

13: The firing held very sharp. The ships came up the river.

All the American batteries along the East River opened fire on four British warships as they sailed northward. The vessels, which disdainfully refused to fire a single return shot, were HMS *Phoenix* and HMS *Roebuck*, forty-four guns each, the thirty-two-gun HMS *Orpheus*, and the twenty-eight-gun HMS *Carysfort*.

> 14: The Regulars were in continual motion at night. It was thought they would make an attack in the morning. Cannon roared.
> 15 [Sunday]: S.Day. The Regulars landed in York; had a hot battle. We had to retreat. I lay out in the field; the earth was our bed, and the heavens our covering.

On 15 September, British landing craft finally poured their troops over American defenses weakened by incessant bombardment. The enemy flank attack caused a precipitous American retreat up the west side of Manhattan Island. The mass withdrawal did not stop until Washington's (again) miraculously preserved army was safe behind fortifications-in-depth on Washington Heights. The following morning (as we have seen in *Chapter IV*), the commander in chief ordered out a scouting party to discover just how far the enemy had advanced during the previous afternoon and evening.

> 16: About 100 of us engaged 2,000; the enemy drove us. I was shot through my arm. Went off over King's Bridge.

In one second, Obadiah was out of the fighting.

> 17: I went to the hospital. Felt pretty hurt. Heard two men died there.

At that time, there was no medical corps in the revolutionary army. Hospitals were improvised and without trained nurses— Florence Nightingale was not born until 1820.

> 18: My arm was painful, but I felt hearty.
> 19: It was swollen very badly, but most of us were comfortable.

20: My wound swelled worse. Nehemiah and Robert Cleveland came to see me, with my Captain and some of our company. A wounded man died at night.
21: I saw Dr. Fitch. Heard Brother Waldo was coming here. A piece of bone came out of my arm. York was burnt.

On 21 September, a great fire, fed by high winds, destroyed over 300 homes and buildings in New York City. The enemy blamed American spies, like captured Ranger Captain Nathan Hale, for the conflagration. Whether arson or accident, the cause of the fire has never been established. As far back as July, many officers in the Continental Army had urged destruction of the city, but Congress vehemently refused permission.

22: I moved from the hospital, about a mile. Slept none all night. Another battle with the Regulars. Colonel Jackson wounded.

Howe, continuing to test the American defenses on upper Manhattan, also prepared to outflank Washington's army by landing troops on the eastern shore of Westchester County. The makeshift army field hospital where Obadiah lay was in lower Westchester.

23: Waldo came to see me. My arm pained me very much. No sleep at night hardly.

The arrival of his brother at camp, only a week after Obadiah was wounded, was fortuitous. There was never enough help in the army hospitals to properly care for patients. The assistance and emotional support of a family member was invaluable.

24: No news. My arm was very painful. No sleep at night.
25: A doctor drummed out of the camp. I slept well at night. The swelling went down some.
26: My arm was very bad. Swelled very bad again, but my heart did not fail me.
27: No news. My arm was very bad.
28: I moved to Eastchester. Had nothing done to my arm. Slept none to speak of at night; though it was hard times. My arm was near as big as my thigh.
29 [Sunday]: S.Day. I thought my arm must be cut off, but lived in hope. It was bathed, and eased it some. Slept pretty well at night.

Obadiah's apprehension was justified. Until the late 19th century, amputation to prevent the spread of gangrene and resulting death was standard medical practice for badly injured limbs. That Obadiah kept his arm was due only to the lack of military surgeons.

> 30: A bath and poultice was applied to it, which abated the swelling wonderfully. I thought the Lord called aloud to me, in causing the swelling to abate in such a manner.
> October 1: I was well as to health, but my arm pulled off my flesh fast.
> 2: It was somewhat cold. My arm was very comfortable. I was thankful to think there was any hope of saving my arm.
> 3: My arm was cut open, which was very hard to bear, but nothing to what I deserve to bear for my sins, which are many.
> 4: My arm was very stiff and sore. It wasn't undone for fear of bleeding.
> 5: Nothing done to my arm. It was very sore and stiff.
> 6 [Sunday]: S.Day. My arm was dressed. It had a doleful hole in it. Smelled dreadfully.
> 7: I was pretty hearty. My arm was very sore but better, as I could see.
> 8: No news. My arm was comfortable, etc.
> 9: Daniel Osgood died. Three ships and three tenders went up the North River; the heaviest cannonading that ever I heard.

As he begins to recover, Obadiah is once more interested in and listening for news from Forts Washington and Lee on the banks of the Hudson River, eleven miles away. On 9 October, HMS *Phoenix*, HMS *Roebuck*, and HMS *Tartar*, with tenders, fought their way past the river forts into the Tappan Zee. In their third encounter with HMS *Phoenix* in as many months, the aim of the American gunners improved; all the enemy ships' rigging was severely damaged, one officer was killed, and twenty-six sailors were wounded. The action convinced Howe that Fort Washington, which until then had been bypassed, must be taken.

> 10: Dull weather. My arm was very painful and sore, but I could stir my fingers and bend my elbow some.
> 11: My arm was very sore and painful at night. There was a frost.
> 12: The Regulars landed on the mainland. Heard some firing.

Howe finally began his Long Island Sound flank attack on Washington's army in Westchester County with an unsuccessful landing at narrow Throg's Neck, ten miles south of Eastchester. Howe's entire 13,000-man operation was temporarily pinned down by the stout defense of Colonel Edward Hand and twenty-five Pennsylvania riflemen.

13 [Sunday]: S.Day. Very pleasant weather. My arm was better.
14: I moved from Eastchester to go to [New] Jersey. Went to my regiment, and heard Ebenezer Simonds and Daniel Kendall were dead.

As 13,000 Americans retreated towards White Plains, their line of march passed near Eastchester. Obadiah, now a member of the "walking wounded," made his way to see old friends.

15: I saw Gageborough men and heard of home. Went back to Eastchester again.
16: A great movement with our army. We were ordered to move to Connecticut.
17: A cloudy day. My arm was very comfortable.
18: We moved to New Rochelle. The Regulars landed close by where we were. We moved to the Saw Pits [Port Chester]. The cannon and small arms roared pretty smart.

As some of Howe's troops came ashore at Pell's Point, less than five miles below New Rochelle, 750 Continentals under Colonel John Glover markedly slowed the enemy's progress, killing four and wounding twenty. Eight Americans were killed and thirteen wounded.

19: We went on our journey; got to Horseneck [Greenwich] in Connecticut. My arm was getting better very slow.
20 [Sunday]: S.day. We moved to Horseneck Meeting House. No doctor to dress our wounds.
21: Cannon and small arms roared very sharp.
22: No great news. Waldo was sick.
23: I went to see Waldo. He was very poor, and discouraged that he never would get well. I was concerned about him. My arm grew worse.
24: My arm grew worse still.

25: My arm was cut open to the bone again. I went to see Brother again; he was better. My arm was painful at night.

26: I had my arm cut open on the other side, almost four inches. The doctor ran his fingers through my arm and pulled out two pieces of bone. Such pain I never underwent before in my life, but nothing to what I deserve.

Anesthesia was seventy years in the future.

27 [Sunday]: S.Day. Another piece of bone came out of my arm. I went to see my brother; he was better. The cannon roared very hard. We sunk two ships.

At White Plains, only seven miles west of Greenwich, Howe's massed artillery attempted to soften the American defenses in preparation for an all-out assault on 28 October. Each side numbered about 13,000 men. The pitched battle on the following day, in which 313 of the enemy were killed, was a standoff. Twenty-five Americans died and 125 were wounded. The British retained possession of the field for more than a week before returning to New York City.

28: A hot battle at White Plains. Our people stood them off. I sent a letter to Father, etc.

29: I went to see Waldo. He was almost well.

30: My arm was better; the doctor said it looked nicely. I was not well.

31: Two pieces of bone taken out of my arm. The doctor said it would be stiff.

November 1: I was very poor, with pain in my head and bones.

2: I kept to my room, I was so poor.

3 [Sunday]: S.Day. I was better, so I went out.

4: I set out to go and see Waldo. I was so weak I had to come back.

5: I was better. It was very pleasant weather.

6: I went to see Waldo. He had gone home. Very warm weather indeed. My arm was getting better fast.

7: I had a very fine walk in the fields. The weather was very pleasant.

8: We heard the Regulars had left White Plains.

9: Regular and Tory prisoners went by here; 17 of them.

10 [Sunday]: S.Day. I was very poor, with a pain in my hips, knees, and ankles.

11: I remained very poor.
12: My fever seemed to abate. I was very sore. Slept none all night, hardly.
13: I was so poor and weak that I staggered as I went about.
14: I was better, so I went out of doors.
15: I saw Colonel Cleveland; heard Waldo had got home.
16: I felt better. Now two months since I was wounded. This day Fort Washington was taken.

Against his better judgment, Washington accepted the counsel of some of his generals and retained possession of Fort Washington, the last remaining American stronghold in New York City. On 16 November, with the fort's many shortcomings betrayed by a traitor, William Demont, the fortification and its outworks fell before an overwhelming British and German attack. Private John Corbin with the First Pennsylvania Artillery was mortally wounded at the side of his gun; his twenty-five-year-old wife Margaret replaced him until she, too, was grievously injured (see *Chapter VII*). In the frigid weather, the Hessian captors began stripping the defenders of their outer clothing, but the British commander put a stop to that particular practice. The loss of a quarter of the Continental Army—with artillery, arms, ammunition, and war materiel—in a single afternoon, was a devastating blow to patriot morale. It also brought Washington's leadership into question with Congress.

17 [Sunday]: S.Day. I felt pretty well.
18: I went a mile and a half and back again.
19: I felt very well. The weather was very pleasant.
20: The men from Canterbury went home. It was cloudy warm weather.

A strategic problem in the early years of the Revolution was the lack of conformity in enlistment periods. They ranged from three or six months to a year, depending on state and local assessments of the existing military situation. Two hastily prepared and critical operations, one unsuccessful (the attack on Quebec City) and the other successful (crossing the Delaware), were both triggered by expiring (New Year's Eve) enlistments. As the war lengthened, so did the required periods of service, which Congress eventually made "for the duration." The familiar boyhood friends Obadiah encountered as

they passed through Greenwich on their way home to Canterbury
were probably 1775 enlistees whose year was up.

21: Rainy loury [gloomy] weather, and very warm.
22: Rainy weather and very warm.
23: Cloudy, dull weather. My arm was getting better very slowly.
24 [Sunday] S.Day. Warm, foggy weather.
25: No news to write. The weather very dull.
26: Rainy weather. I was not well. No news from the army.

Where was the army? On the march through New Jersey towards
the Delaware River. A week earlier, Cornwallis's troops had crossed
the Hudson, causing a hasty evacuation of Fort Lee. All its stockpiled
military stores were abandoned. Five Americans were killed and 100
"skulkers" were captured. These were, as Thomas Paine scribbled
during that shivering march, "the times that try men's souls."

27: Dull loury weather. Cleared off at night.
28: I thought I should feel better if I were at home, for winter was
coming on and there I should have a good fire to set by, and
somebody to take care of me.
29: Cold nights but pleasant days. I saw two men from Sutton's.
He and his family were well. I was not well.
30: I was taken sick with a pain in my head and back.
December 1 [Sunday]: S.Day. My fever increased. I grew worse.
2: Very cold. I was very sick. No sleep at night.
3: I was very sick. Had no stomach to eat anything.
4: I was so sick that I could hardly stand alone.
5: I was somewhat better. It was Thanksgiving Day,[3] and such a
one I never saw before; none of my friends was near me. A Negro
died at night.
6: A dull & loury day.
7: Chilly, cloudy weather. I felt very dull, but kept stirring about.
8: I was on the mending hand. The weather was very warm for this
time of year.
9: Fine weather. My arm was so well, I took the sling off and let it
hang down. It was very stiff and sore.

[3] Thanksgiving then was celebrated by individual gubernatorial proclamation in each
colony and state. Not until 1863 did Abraham Lincoln establish it as a national
holiday, and it was only in 1941 that Congress fixed Thanksgiving Day as the last
Thursday in November.

10: Chilly, cloudy weather.
11: Cloudy, cold weather; looked like snow. The snow fell two inches deep at night.
12: Warm weather; the snow went off.
13: Fine weather. We heard our army had defeated the Regulars, and took a great number.

Washington's terribly diminished army was now safely over the Delaware. Skirmishing, however, continued in New Jersey; on 13 December, enemy cavalrymen, including a young private named Banastre Tarleton (see *Chapter VIII*)—captured General Lee and his staff asleep in a tavern at Basking Ridge, New Jersey.

14: I set out to go to Peekskill. Went six miles.

Peekskill, twenty-six miles northwest of Greenwich on the Hudson River, was an important Westchester County military command post and encampment. The British having withdrawn, Obadiah was able to cross middle Westchester in three days without hindrance. At Peekskill, he could be formally discharged from the Continental Army.

15 [Sunday]: S.day. Went through North Castle [six miles] and Cortlandt Manor [eight miles]. Stayed all night.
16: Went to Peekskill [six miles]. Heared General Lee and his life guard was taken.
17: My arm broke, and ran terribly. It was very sore. I put a poultice on at night.
18: Cold weather, but a good fire at the mouth of the tent kept me warm.
19: Very cold weather. My arm was very bad.
20: Snowed almost all day. My arm was better.
21: A piece of lead worked through my arm, almost half an inch long.
22 [Sunday]: S.Day. Cold weather. No news.
23: My arm broke on the other side. It felt easy.
24: Fine weather, but almost too cold for comfort to live in tents.
25: Christmas Day. Very clear, cold weather. No news worth a-writing.
26: Snowed all day. Cleared off at night.

On Christmas Day, in a snowstorm moving northeast, Washington recrossed the ice-choked Delaware with the 2,400 men that were left of his army. Early on the morning of 26 December, the Americans attacked a 1,400-man German garrison occupying Trenton, New Jersey, killing and wounding 105 and capturing 918. The Hessian commander was killed. Only four Americans were killed and four wounded. With this unexpected turn of events, Washington's reputation as a military leader was restored.

> 27: Clear and pleasant after the storm. My arm was getting better.
> 28: Cloudy, dull weather; looked like snow. No news. I thought if I were at home, I would not enlist again till my arm got well.
> 29: [Sunday]: S.Day. Cold weather.
> 30: I set out from Peekskill; came up [eighteen miles] to Fishkill through towns' names I do not know.
> 31: We set out, Jonathan Hill and I, from Fishkill. Came nine miles.

It was a cold and cheerless New Year's Eve on the 124-mile road home to Gageborough. On New Year's Day 1777, Obadiah, still in pain, became a statistic; one among the 562 American soldiers wounded (604 were killed) in the War of Independence during the year 1776.

> January 1: We came through part of Poughkeepsie into the Nine Partners [Grant] [sixteen miles]. The weather was very loury and dull, and bad traveling.
> 2: We came 14 miles.
> 3: We came 15 miles.
> 4: Came out of Nine Partners, through Salisbury [Connecticut], into Sheffield; which was 14 miles.
> 5 [Sunday]: S.Day. Came through [Great] Barrington and Stockbridge into Lenox [twenty-one miles].

So close to home, Obadiah, now probably slogging alone, ignored any stricture on Lord's Day travel.

> 6: Came through Pittsfield, and came home [seventeen miles]; and felt glad of it.

*DESPITE HIS* bone-shattering experience, Obadiah was not quite through with George III—nor was the King yet done with him. Although Obadiah's arm was healing, it was some time before he could again load, raise, and fire a musket.[4]

As Obadiah reached home at Gageborough (and apparently discontinued his journal), Lord George Germain's ministry, working in London from large-scale maps that made extended troop movement seem easy,[5] was formulating a grand new four-pronged military campaign to crush the rebellion once and for all. To split New England from the other states down the line of the Hudson River, the coordinated plan called for a portion of the British occupation force in New York City to strike south at Philadelphia, the heart of the revolutionary government.

That mission accomplished, along with the destruction of Washington's southern armies *en passant*, the British strike force was to return to New York to mount a fresh offensive up the Hudson River to join another army driving east from Fort Niagara through the Mohawk Valley. Still another army would retrace Sir Guy Carleton's thwarted 1776 invasion route south from Montreal.

The scheme was ambitious and complicated. Coordination was to fail in every particular save one, the occupation of Philadelphia, which continued far longer than the War Office had intended and

---

[4] A recent Surgeon General of the United States, obliged the author with a diagnosis of Obadiah's wound and the 18th century army medical care he was able to obtain:

It appears that Private Brown sustained a penetrating wound of the arm (probably his upper arm) resulting in an open, comminuted fracture of the humerus, with some retention of the missile (lead slug). Probably no emergency treatment, except a wound dressing, was received. A wound infection rapidly developed, localized in approximately two weeks, at which time an incision and drainage was done. A chronic infection of the bone marrow (osteomyelitis) developed at the fracture site, as evidenced by frequent extrusion of pieces of devitalized bone from the wound, formation of abscesses, fever, malaise, and probable loss of weight. Part of the foreign body (lead slug) which was finally extruded from the wound, served as an excellent nidus of infection. It cannot be certain that Private Brown had completely recovered when he reenlisted, since remissions and exacerbations are common in chronic osteomyelitis.

[5] As early as 1775, one enterprising Fleet Street map engraver published a "six-pack" cavalryman's North American *Holster Atlas*, in which a single map covered 660,000 square miles.

eventually led to Sir William Howe's dismissal as commander in chief.[6]

In Montreal, General Carleton, a skilled officer smarting from Lord Germain's rebuke for his "supine" failure to attack Fort Ticonderoga in 1776, was left behind to organize supply lines and guard against another possible revolutionary invasion of Canada through northern New England.

Command of the new 7,173-man army of Regulars, active tories, and German and Native American mercenaries—accompanied by almost 2,000 women and children—went to Carleton's posturing associate, General John Burgoyne. The fifty-five-year-old Burgoyne had sucesssfully lobbied for the job during a quick trip to London, capitalizing on his reputation as a histrionic hero of the Seven Years' War.

Burgoyne's first official act was to issue a manifesto aimed at anyone opposing passage of the King's troops. It promised "devastation, famine and every concomitant horror that a reluctant but indispensable prosecution of military duty must occasion." In his spare time, Burgoyne wrote plays.[7]

ON 18 JUNE 1777, Burgoyne's barges, loaded with troops, finally moved down Lake Champlain. Other units kept pace on shore. At Crown Point, the force reunited and pushed by land towards Fort Ticonderoga.

Since 1755, when the French built the post as Fort Carillon, and through two decades of frontal assault, no one had ever seriously considered the possibility that a few enemy cannon, hauled by hand to the top of a nearby mountain, could command the entire work. On 5 July, British General William Phillips did just that. As darkness fell, the realistic Revolutionaries evacuated Ticonderoga, without firing a shot.[8]

---

[6] The British leader preferred spending the winter months of 1777-78 in the comfortable homes of Philadelphians, rather than languishing in half-burned New York.

[7] A century and more later, another British dramatist, Bernard Shaw, portrayed Burgoyne—in *The Devil's Disciple*—as a sophisticated antihero. Shaw's witty work premiered in New York in 1897. It is the only literate dramatic effort to date to reflect the politics and passions of the American Revolution.

[8] The following year, General Philip Schuyler, who had commanded American

Burgoyne was now less than 100 miles from Albany. Two days later, by overrunning Fort Ann, a dilapidated relic of the French and Indian War at the southernmost tip of Lake Champlain, he was thirty miles nearer his goal. But the next twenty miles to Fort Edward on the upper Hudson wound through some of the most difficult terrain ever traversed by a 7,000-man army. Schuyler, although ailing, was determined to make Burgoyne's route as impassable as possible.

From Fort Edward on 9 July, the American commander ordered Brigadier General John Fellows to "begin as near Fort Ann as possible and fell trees across every road, making the obstructions as effectual as possible, taking up every bridge, and burning the covering and timber."

The following day Schuyler wrote to Washington: "I will throw every obstacle in the enemy's route that I can." Along the narrow forest track through deep defiles and mucky swamps, a thousand Revolutionary soldiers went to work to slow the enemy advance. They dropped trees, flooded bogs, and destroyed causeways and bridges with such success that it took three critical weeks for Burgoyne's advance guard to finally break out onto the banks of the Hudson eighteen miles north of Saratoga.

*AT GAGEBOROUGH* meanwhile, "Gentleman Johnny" Burgoyne's swaggering manifesto brought Obadiah back into action, along with militiamen from every Green Mountain and Berkshire hamlet and farm within a hundred miles of Fort Edward. They all came flocking to join the Northern Department army, now commanded by General Horatio Gates.

Burgoyne reached Fort Edward on 30 July 1777. One would think Private Brown had seen enough fighting and wounding for one war. By 14 August Obadiah had enlisted again, and was on a forced march to Bennington, Vermont, with other members of Captain William Clark's newly formed militia company of Gageborough. If he began and kept another wartime diary, it is lost. The Gageborough soldiers covered the thirty-five miles to their destination in time to

---

forces at Ticonderoga, requested a court martial to put to rest rumors of incompetence, or worse, in the loss of the Fort. He was honorably acquitted; the record showed he had pleaded in vain for American fortification of the strategic mount.

join with 2,000 other Americans in the one-sided Battle of Bennington on 16 August.

Revolutionary disgust with the tories and their mercenary allies
boiled over, reaching a battle pitch not matched until King's Mountain three years later. Like their Southern "over-the- mountain"
counterparts, the Green Mountain Boys played for keeps; although
Regular prisoners were not harmed, the disposal of particularly
obnoxious tory neighbors kept on well after the battle was over.
Obadiah came through his second engagement without a scratch, but
saw fifty of his companions wounded and thirty killed. The two large
foraging detachments from Burgoyne's army suffered badly: 200
were killed and 696 captured.

Obadiah served only through 21 August, but he was there when
he was needed. He missed the further fighting at Saratoga and, on 17
October, the momentous surrender of Burgoyne's entire army,
which effectively guaranteed the absolutely essential French Alliance.

IN THE FIRST United States census, in 1790, Obadiah Brown is listed
as a resident of Cambridge, New York, Albany County, thirty miles
northwest of his old home town of Gageborough. Obadiah, at the
ripe old age of thirty-seven, is shown as "1-1-3," indicating himself,
his wife (Lucy?), a son under 16, and two daughters.

With the Revolution won and now far behind him, Obadiah, like
any American, was busy raising a family, and struggling to move
himself and the country ahead.

# CHAPTER VII

# Women at War

*IN WHICH dedicated female revolutionaries demonstrate unswerving allegiance to ideals of freedom—while one woman chooses another course.*

*IN THE* American Revolution, only a few women ever pulled a trigger or helped fire a cannon. The times frowned on such behavior from its females, which is not to say that the critical part they played in the struggle went unnoticed or unacknowledged. A century and a half ago, when memories still were green, one biographer easily named 171 notable women in a three-volume *Women of the American Revolution*.

Maintaining the home front was demanding. Women's duties included collecting urine for gunpowder processing; spinning, weaving, and sewing clothing and uniforms; preparing cartridges and bandages; along with all the other normal chores of farm and town—now made infinitely harder by the absence of their husbands and sons in the army.

Not every female stayed home. Throughout the war, many women and children lived in army camps, having accompanied their men when they joined the army, rather than stay in areas like Long Island and lower Westchester County occupied by the enemy. Amid all his other concerns, Washington fought a losing battle in keeping them out of his supply and baggage wagons. These American camp women performed mundane but essential tasks—including cooking, sewing and darning, and bearing and raising children—on the march.

Usually viewed by general officers as a necessary encumbrance, the numbers of these hard-working, ration-consuming women (and children) varied with each turn in the fortunes of war. On both sides, they amounted to from five to ten percent of the total camp population. Aside from the inevitable presence of a handful of "white-stockinged women," like those Obadiah Brown saw drummmed out of Cambridge Camp, most women followers were tolerated and ignored. Only during army movement were camp and town populations kept as far apart as possible.

For example, on 4 August 1777, with his army poised outside Philadelphia, Washington forbade any more women to come into camp and sought to expel many of those already there: "In the present state of the army, every encumbrance proves prejudicial. The multitude of women in particular, especially those who are pregnant, or have children, are a clog upon every movement."

Three weeks later, Washington led 9,000 Continental officers and men down Broad Street through the newly liberated capital of the republic, past wildly cheering throngs of Philadelphians. At the same time, a separate, very different parade of camp women and their children slowly snaked its way through the city's emptied stableyards, alleys, and back streets. Washington's order had been simple: "Not a woman belonging to the army is to be seen."

FOLLOWING BRITISH North American military tradition going back to General Edward Braddock and the French and Indian Wars, the enemy camps, too, contained a large number of women and children, usually in excess of the commander in chief's stipulated and standard quota of six women to each company of thirty-eight men and nine officers. A 1777 British army ration return for eleven regiments indicated a total of 22,068 men, as well as 1,648 camp women (on half ration) and their 539 children (on quarter ration). The women and children accounted for close to nine percent of the total camp population.

Women and children were everywhere. In New York City in 1779, the 4,000-man British garrison was accompanied by 1,550 women and 968 children. During the enemy occupation of Newport, mercenary General Friedrich von Wurmb criticized his command with understandable hyperbole: "This corps has more women and children than men, which causes considerable vexation."

A British historian once remarked—without a smile—that the American Revolution was the handiwork of a clever and well-organ-

ized group of white male Protestant radicals, who won independence
for the United States even though only a third of the colonial
population was with them. Although, among that Revolutionary
third, there were just as many fervent females as males, it was the men
who predominated and ran things. Only on the rarest of occasions
did a woman with the army have the opportunity to fire a gun.
Nonetheless, three women did break the mold, either through circumstance or determination. All three of them fired at the enemy.
The new United States eventually demonstrated its gratitude by
awarding each of them a modest military pension—and in one
husband's case, the first U.S. pension benefit continuation to a
veteran's male spouse.

*WE SHOULD PROPERLY BEGIN* by marveling at the incredible decep-
tion of Deborah Sampson, born at Plympton in eastern Massachusetts 17 December 1760. Named after her mother, Deborah Bradford
Sampson, young Deborah possessed worthy New England antece-
dents, and never tired of mentioning her great-grandfather, the Bay
Colony's first governor.

Deborah's mother and father Jonathan were the poorest relations
of the Bradford clan. Robert Shurtleff Sampson, eldest of the five
children born to the impoverished family, died; while Jonathan
straggled off to Maine looking for work and was never heard from
again.

The family fell apart as the children, according to custom, were
bound out to neighbors. As a strong and vigorous teenager in the
home of a local deacon, Deborah expected little from her future life
except work as an indentured servant or, if lucky, a substitute
schoolteacher and marriage to some farmer.

But by the time Deborah was fifteen, the spring breeze of the
Revolution was blowing in Massachusetts. Her elder brother
Ephraim, dressed in an ill-fitting militiaman's uniform, rushed north
a few miles to the siege of Boston. Later he would begin a series of
letters about army life all over the Northeast that continued through
the first five years of the war. Probably it was the excitement in those
letters that impelled Deborah to turn her life inside out.

On an April day in 1781, this quiet, self-reliant, broad-shoul-
dered, twenty-one-year-old substitute schoolteacher cropped her

blond hair, pulled on a man's trousers, assumed a man's name, and volunteered for three years in the Continental Army.

Her disguise was adequate; it was the enlistment bounty that did her in. To celebrate her new career "with the boys," Deborah got expensively well-oiled at a local tavern. By the end of the evening, her secret was out, and she fled into the night, technically a bounty jumper.

But Deborah Sampson was an unusually tenacious woman. At a Worcester, Massachusetts, recruiting station, wearing the same baggy men's clothes, and this time using the name of her deceased sibling, Robert Shurtleff, she tried to reenlist and succeeded, joining Captain George Webb's Company of the 4th Massachusetts Regiment. This time, and for the thirty months of her enlistment to come, she stayed out of tippling houses.

By 13 May 1781, Robert was stationed at West Point, pulling guard duty in her government issue uniform, which she described in her published memoirs:[1]

> A blue coat lined with white, with white wings on the shoulders and cords, and on the arms and pockets; a white waistcoat, breeches or overalls, and stockings with black straps above the knee; half boots; a black stock; and a cap with a variegated cockade on one side, a plumed tip with red on the other, and a white sash about the crown.

Robert and her comrades saw far-flung service during these closing years of the Revolution. They marched as far south as Maryland and Virginia to help compel Cornwallis's surrender at Yorktown. By the spring of 1782, they were back wrestling with the British and their allies for control of Westchester County. Robert was now called "Smockface," and, due to her lack of beard, "The Blooming Boy." But no one penetrated her disguise, even after she was wounded by tory partisans near Tarrytown, New York. Luckily, the saber cut on her head was a scratch, providing an excuse for trimming her hair even shorter.

---

[1] Ghost-written and inevitably embroidered, published in Dedham, Massachusetts, in 1796, under the title, *The Female Review, or Memoirs of an American Young Lady whose Life and Character are Peculiarly Distinguished, being a Continental Soldier for nearly Three Years in the Late American War.*

Robert's second wound, in a skirmish near Eastchester, New York, was a more serious problem. Assisted to a French Army field hospital, she was forced to use a penknife to privately extract an enemy musket ball lodged in her thigh. The subsequent infection left her limping for the rest of her life.

By the end of 1782, Robert was sufficiently recovered to ride on a wagon when the 4th Massachusetts was posted to Fort Ticonderoga. Because of her wound, she was soon moved to Philadelphia as an orderly to Massachusetts General John Paterson.

Struck down in the peaceful summer of 1783 by a fever that almost killed her, Robert relates in her memoirs that she was carried to the home of a Dr. Binney, who immediately discovered Robert's sex, but was willing to keep the secret. It was Binney's niece who created an unforeseen contretemps. Aggressively pursuing her uncle's immobilized patient, she finally uncovered the charade.

Deciding that Deborah's interests now were best served by candor, Dr. Binney went directly to her commander, General Paterson. He did discharge Robert from the service on 23 October 1783, but sent her off (in women's clothes) to Washington at New Windsor, New York, with a letter of praise. Washington enjoyed few good laughs during the Revolution; this must have been one of them.

Washington gave Deborah some money, a letter of advice (unfortunately lost forever), and an escort home to Plympton. A year after the war, on 7 April 1784, she married thirty-year-old Benjamin Gannett, a farmer from Sharon, Massachusetts, twenty-five miles northeast of Plympton. Gannett had served briefly in the state militia; Deborah was the army veteran of the family. She bore Benjamin three children. The Massachusetts legislature voted Deborah a special $150 bonus, with a note of commendation for "preserving the virtue and chastity of her sex unblemished."

But Deborah Sampson Gannett was not one to sit around waiting for government entitlements. In 1802, at forty-two, she decided to start capitalizing on her already considerable fame. She created a two-act show and took it on the road, leaving Benjamin at home with the kids. She traveled alone through New England and New York, booking halls in which she recounted the story of her wartime service. Her first appearance, in nearby Boston, netted Deborah seven dollars.

Farther west, she enjoyed a lengthy visit with General Paterson, now a New York judge. The 31 August 1802 newspaper advertisement for her Albany, New York, performance, under the headline "MRS. GANNETT'S EXHIBITION," read:

> The Ladies and Gentlemen of Albany and its vicinity are respectfully informed that Mrs. Gannett, the Celebrated American Heroine who served nearly three years with great reputation in our Revolutionary Army, will, at the request of a number of respectable characters, deliver an Address to the inhabitants of this city at the Courthouse this evening at half-past seven o'clock. Tickets may be had at the Courthouse from five o'clock until the performance begins. Price: 25c. Children half price.

In every city, Deborah was an enormous, held-over success, in a day when there was as yet no lecture circuit. After recounting her military adventures, she retired offstage, to reappear dressed in her faded regimentals and carrying a musket. Then she shouted her way through Baron von Steuben's old *Manual of Arms*. This brought down the house. For a while at least, Deborah—who kept the most careful accounting of all her expenses and income, down to the last penny ("For brushing off seats, 17c")—rode high.

In 1804, sixty-nine-year-old Paul Revere petitioned his Congressman for a war veteran's pension for Mrs. Gannett, writing that

> When I heard her spoken of as a soldier, I formed the idea of a tall, masculine female who had a small share of understanding, without education, and one of the meanest of her sex. When I saw and discoursed with her, I was agreeably surprised to find a small, effeminate, and conversable woman whose education entitled her to a better situation in life.

On 11 March 1805, under additional pressure from Judge Paterson on Deborah's behalf, the U.S. Government granted her a disabled veteran's pension at the standard rate of four dollars a month, retroactive to the date of her application twenty-six months earlier. Under a cost of living Pension Act revision thirteen years later, in 1818, the monthly payment was increased to eight dollars.[2]

---

[2] Although everyone knew who she was, Deborah was required to swear under oath to her thirty months of military service in a special affidavit; her old adversary, the British Army, had burned all the pertinent War Office records in Washington in 1814.

Deborah Gannet, the "American Heroine," still limping at sixty-seven and in increasing pain from her war wound, died in straitened circumstances 29 April 1827. Four years later, taking advantage of new pension legislation, seventy-seven-year-old Benjamin Gannett, "representing himself as infirm in health, and destitute, with two daughters dependent on charity for support," applied for a "veteran's surviving-spouse pension" of ninety-six dollars a year. To underline his need, Benjamin produced an old doctor's bill to Deborah for $600, which he had paid.

It took Congress six more years to respond favorably to Benjamin's application. During Christmas week 1837, the House Committee on Revolutionary Pensions, noting that "the whole history of the American Revolution records no other case like this," recommended granting Benjamin a pension for life of eighty dollars a year, plus a retroactive lump sum of $540.

Congress, as usual, was late. The "American Heroine's" husband had died the previous week.

*MARGARET COCHRAN* was born in Franklin County, Pennsylvania, in 1751. She grew up accustomed to the hard vicissitudes of frontier life. When she was four years old, her Scotch-Irish immigrant father was killed and scalped by Iroquois natives striking south into the upper Susquehanna River country from their settlements in central New York. The Iroquois did not kill enemy women, but carried Margaret's mother off into permanent captivity. Margaret was elsewhere during the raid, and so was left to be raised by relatives.

She was twenty-one years old when she met and married John Corbin, a transplanted Virginian living on the Pennsylvania frontier. She was twenty-five when her artilleryman husband died by her side in an outlying redoubt (Fort Tryon) during the British attack on Fort Washington in New York City 16 November 1776. Already a woman of independent spirit and proven courage, Margaret moved Corbin's body aside to take command of his cannon until she, too, was struck down by enemy grapeshot. Her arm was nearly severed and her breast badly mangled.

Margaret was hospitalized by the British in New York. She convalesced slowly, never recovering full use of her arm. Her status as a prisoner confused everyone. She was sent to Philadelphia in 1777, where she was paroled and then assigned to the Continental invalid corps, in which she remained until formally mustered out of the army in 1783.

Margaret Cochran Corbin became the first woman in the United States to whom Congress voted (6 July 1779) a military pension—half her dead husband's pay for the twenty-one years remaining in her life. In a further demonstration of government generosity in the middle of a costly war, Congress also voted her a complete set of new clothes.

After the Revolution, Margaret Corbin settled in the Hudson River hamlet of Highland Falls, New York, just below what would become the United States Military Academy at West Point. Now in her mid-forties, she had become not only a living legend, but an impossibly bibulous harridan as well, known familiarly among the locals as "Captain Molly" (inevitably leading to her being confused with "Molly Pitcher") or, behind her back, as "Dirty Kate." Margaret died in 1800. A century later her remains were transferred from Highland Falls to the government cemetery at West Point, where they were placed beneath a modest monument.

*IT TURNED OUT* to be the longest sustained day's action of the Revolution. It also was one of the hottest, where the heat of the day certainly matched the heat of the battle. The desperate struggle on 28 June 1778 against man and the sun raged near Monmouth Court House in interior New Jersey. With the temperature at ninety-six degrees in the shade, thirty-seven Continentals and fifty-nine enemy soldiers died of heat exhaustion.

The full-scale contest between Washington's and Sir Henry Clinton's armies was precipitated by advance units of the 5,400-man American army, marching eastward with fourteen fieldpieces from Valley Forge, under the detached command of General Charles Lee. The group soon overtook Cornwallis's rear guard of the twelve-mile-long 10,000-man British column, its progress slowed by 3,000 evacuated Philadelphia tories. The enemy was in retreat overland to New York City, having left Philadelphia ten days earlier.

The ensuing struggle was long and costly to both sides. In the swirl of heat and dust, the British lost 251 dead and 170 wounded. American losses were 119 dead—including the sunstroke victims—and 161 wounded. "I presume everyone has heard of the heat of that day," reminisced "Private Yankee Doodle" Joseph Plumb Martin, "but none can realize it, that did not feel it." On such a day in such a battle, the need for water on both sides—to drink and to cool the overheated artillery—was paramount.

Among the many striking events of this last major encounter of the Revolution in the North were Washington's unusually vituperative battlefield sacking of the bungling obstructionist General Lee and the instant cannonization of Mary Ludwig Hays[3]

Mary Hays was a rowdy, engaging thirty-four-year-old Pennsylvania Dutchwoman, who, after the Battle of Monmouth, came to be known to all Americans as "Molly Pitcher." (Later in the war, the name came to be applied to any camp woman who carried water to parched or wounded soldiers.)

Mary Hays had gone to Valley Forge to be with her husband John, an artillery private in the 7th Pennsylvania Regiment. On that scorching day at Monmouth, Molly filled and carried water buckets, standard equipment for wetting the large sponge on a staff used to quench glowing cartridge fragments in the cannon barrel after discharge. As the story was first told, Mary Hays's husband John fell from a wound (or sunstruck) at the side of his overheated cannon. Molly continued to help serve the gun, swabbing, loading, ramming, aiming, and firing. But as with Betsy Ross, the real person was soon obscured by the myth. By the beginning of the 20th century, revisionist historians were chattering away about her "tarnished reputation," calling Molly an "uneducated woman who drank, chewed tobacco, and swore like a trooper."

No wonder a group of Philadelphia society matrons reportedly "thanked their lucky stars when certain contemporary testimony was brought to their attention, and caused them to abandon the idea of erecting a civic monument to Molly's memory."

An eyewitness report by Joseph Plumb Martin published in Maine half a century after the battle was probably responsible for her fall from public grace. In his *Narrative of Some of the Adventures, Dangers, and Sufferings of a Revolutionary Soldier*, the irrepressible "Private Yankee Doodle" gossips about the events at Monmouth. He recounts "one little incident in the heat of the cannonade which I think would be unpardonable not to mention":

---

[3] Anglicized from Heis.

A woman attending with her husband at his artillery piece the whole time, and in the act of reaching for a cartridge and having one of her feet as far before the other as she could step, a cannon shot from the enemy passed directly between her legs, without doing any other damage than carrying away all the lower part of her petticoat.

Looking down with apparent unconcern, she observed that it was lucky it did not pass a little higher, for in that case it might have carried away something else—and continued her occupation.

It's easy enough to see why Molly, who lived to be eighty-eight, remains the legendary darling of the United States Artillery, who still toast her memory with a rollicking: ". . .beverage stronger and ever richer/ Than water poured from Molly's pitcher."

*JUST ABOUT* as different from Margaret Cochran Corbin as you can get, but just as feisty, was her fellow Pennsylvanian Margaret Shippen Arnold. This attractive eighteen-year-old Philadelphia coquette was wooed (with shamelessly recycled love letters) and won 8 April 1779 by a man more than twice her age, one of the new nation's greatest generals, Benedict Arnold. Arnold's first wife had died, and his three sons were being raised by his sister Hannah.

Peggy Shippen was the youngest of four daughters of a comfortable, ostensibly neutral Phildelphia family. Her father, Judge Edward Shippen, generally disapproved of the rambunctious Arnold's politics and reputation as a ladykiller. In an age when Americans rarely committed their sexual feelings to paper, Arnold eventually would feel sufficiently secure to describe the pleasures of his new "connubial connexion" to Robert Howe, the general he supplanted at West Point:

> I myself had enjoyed a tolerable share of the dissipated joys of life,[4] as well as the scenes of sensual gratification incident to a man of my nervous constitution. But, when set in competition with those I have since felt and still enjoy, I consider my time of celibacy in some measure misspent.

[4] On his 1775 march through the Kennebec/Chaudiere wilderness to attack Quebec, Arnold shared the trip with Jacatacqua, a young "Abenaki Queen with golden thighs"—particular favorite of the teen-aged expedition member Aaron Burr.

While soliciting Peggy's hand from Judge Shippen, the general had written, "I flatter myself that the time is at hand when our unhappy contest will be at an end, and peace and domestic happiness will be restored to everyone."

But the pressures that would soon estrange Major General Benedict Arnold from the Revolutionary cause and his comrades in arms soon began building. Their genesis was buried in a series of real and fancied legislative and military slights and rebuffs, of which the most galling to Arnold was a lengthy court-martial over his alleged private use of public wagons. He successfully concealed a host of kickback army contracts, while using his position as military governor for personal gain. Only a month after his marriage to Peggy, Arnold was preparing to defect to the forces against which he had fought with conspicuous bravery for four years.

He had an eager and willing partner in his wife. Even if Peggy Shippen did not actually propose the treason (and many thought she did), "it is impossible to doubt," as Carl van Doren insisted in 1941, "that she was not perfectly aware of the conspiracy, from the beginning." Final responsibility for it, of course, must lie with the mature and experienced Arnold, but both he and his wife moved to take advantage of her contact with a friendly enemy, a young adjutant general among the King's troops in New York City, John André.

André was a former prisoner of the Americans captured with Burgoyne at Saratoga, later paroled and exchanged. Serving under Sir William Howe, he had designed the less than modest Turkish harem costumes for the extravagant 3,300-guinea "Mischianza" Ball, and served as its principal coiffeuse. The fete, with British officers and tory belles playing at feudal knights and ladies, was held in Philadelphia 18 May 1778 to mark the departure of Lord Howe as British commander in chief. It was this colorful event that brought André and Peggy Shippen together.

It was an easy matter for Peggy to initiate an innocuous-looking contact between her husband ("Mr. Moore," or "Gustavus"), André ("John Anderson"), and herself (doctoring her letters with invisible ink). In no time, Arnold was dickering with the British over what particular treachery would best serve both parties and how much money would change hands. The enemy's request was simple: unblock the Hudson River and restart the war in the northeast. Arnold would have to insert himself into the West Point command and so weaken its defenses that a British amphibious attack could swallow the post.

Through André and other intermediaries, Arnold was soon deep in ciphered intrigue and negotiations with the British commander in chief, Sir Henry Clinton, to deliver a "blow of importance" to the revolutionary cause. Arnold solicited and received from Washington responsibility for continuing to expand the fortifications at West Point. He located his headquarters in Beverly Robinson's confiscated home across the river near present-day Garrison, New York, in the Hudson highlands.

Among the members of his staff were two aides-de-camp, the recently arrived twenty-seven-year-old Lieutenant Colonel Richard Varick and thirty-three-year-old Major David Salisbury Franks, both of whom were dazzled by Peggy and perceived nothing of the Arnolds' clandestine contacts with the enemy. Franks, an ardent Revolutionary and past president of Montreal's Congregation Shearith Israel,[5] fled Canada in 1776 by volunteering under Arnold, and served with him during subsequent campaigns. Varick had served as an aide to General Philip Schuyler.

At the Robinson House, Arnold was growing restive. He had placed a $100,000 price tag on his treachery, whether successful or not, and the British were balking. Arnold insisted on a covert meeting with Major André to nail down the deal. The two men met past midnight on 22 September 1780 in a pine forest near Haverstraw, New York, where, as a gesture of good faith, Arnold passed along a sheaf of critical military information.

Unfortunately for André, his trip back to the British lines was compromised. The treason was inadvertently revealed with the capture of André, whose boots were filled with the secret papers and maps illustrating the weak spots in West Point's defenses. Confused news of the spy's capture was delivered to Arnold on 25 September 1780 as he, Peggy, Franks, and Varick were enjoying a quiet Monday morning breakfast, awaiting Washington's arrival from Fishkill. Arnold quickly closeted himself for a brief moment with Peggy, then

---

[5] In May 1775, a month after Lexington and Concord, Franks became *persona non grata* after serving a week in the Montreal jail for observing passage of the oppressive Quebec Act by decorating a statue of George III with a necklace of potatoes and the placard, "Behold the Pope of Canada, and the English fool."

leaped on his horse and dashed down Robinson's Lane to an idling military barge. Instead of ordering the crew to pull across the Hudson to West Point, Arnold headed them downstream to the British warship *Vulture*, where they were promptly placed in irons.

Arnold, hero of Quebec, Valcour Island, and Saratoga, had left behind a household in utter confusion. Washington, returning from a Hartford conference with Rochambeau, was expected at any moment. On the ground floor of the Robinson House, Arnold's two aides Varick and Franks wondered how to explain their chief's sudden disappearance. Upstairs in her bedroom, Peggy suddenly began to scream hysterically that red-hot irons were being pressed against her head.

At that moment, Washington, his staff officers, and lifeguard came clattering into the Robinson dooryard. Leaving Franks to deal as best he could with the commander in chief, Varick dashed upstairs, where he found Peggy running half-naked around her bedroom, shouting that her husband was being carried away to heaven, and evildoers were attempting to smother her eighteen-month-old son, Edward.

Varick was thoroughly discomfited, saying later that Peggy's dishabille "was not to be seen even by gentlemen of the family—much less by strangers." Peggy's fit provided a remarkably convincing diversion from the perilous military business at hand. Even Washington was summoned to the bedroom, where Peggy was now diaphanously propped against pillows. He made a vain attempt to restore some household order, but only the arrival of a messenger bearing the incriminating documents brought an end to the uproar and Peggy's charade. Dave R. Palmer, a former Superintendent at the United States Military Acacdemy, has characterized Peggy's performance as "one of the most successful stripteases of all time."

"It was the most affecting scene I was ever witness to," twenty-three-year-old Alexander Hamilton wrote to his bride-to-be Elizabeth Schuyler, daughter of General Schuyler.

> One moment she raved, another she melted into tears, sometimes she pressed her infant to her bosom amd lamented its fate, occasioned by the imprudence of its father, in a manner that would have pierced insensibility itself.

Hamilton's eyewitness account continued:

All the sweetness of beauty, all the loveliness of innocence, all the
tenderness of a wife, and all the fondness of a mother, showed
themselves in her appearance and conduct. We have every reason
to believe that she was entirely unacquainted with the plan, and
that her first knowlege of it was when Arnold went to tell her he
must banish himself from his country, and from her, forever.

The commander in chief's immediate attempt to cut off Arnold's
flight at King's Ferry was too late. The traitor had escaped. In General
Orders on 27 September, Washington broke the news to his army of
the disaffection of a man who had been one of its favorite heroes.
"Treason of the Blackest Dye," Washington told his troops, and
remarked privately to Knox and Lafayette: "Who can we trust now?"

Once the dimensions of Arnold's treachery became known,
suspicion naturally also fell on his two aides as accomplices. The
situation was hardly helped by the arrival of a letter to Washington
from the traitor himself, now resting safely in New York City. In it,
Arnold exonerated Peggy and his two subordinates of any knowledge
of his negotiations with the enemy and innocently inquired whether
it "would be too much of an imposition to ask that my clothes and
baggage may be sent to me."

Gradually the smoke blew away. Close examination by the
commander in chief quickly cleared Varick and Franks of any com-
plicity in Arnold's acts. Peggy, in the courteous custom of the day,
was shipped off by carriage with Franks as escort on 27 September
1780 to her friends and family in Philadelphia, carrying her husband's
clothes and carefully sifted baggage, while "expressing her gratitude
in lively terms" for everyone's "great politeness and humanity."

Washington made an indirect offer to Sir Henry Clinton to trade
Major André for the ex-American general. When the proposal fell on
deaf ears, undoubtedly due to fear of creating a damaging precedent
for cases of future British espionage, André was swiftly hanged.

In Philadelphia, a patriotic mob marked Arnold's treachery by
hauling a farm cart through the city carrying an effigy in full uniform
of a two-faced General Arnold (the faces painted by Charles Willson
Peale). Arnold was being prodded with a pitchfork by the Devil,
while a small boy hidden in the wagon swung the general's head back

and forth. As the cart was dragged through the streets, urchins cavorted around it, chanting:

Major André let a fart,
    Peggy Shippen found it;
Arnold took it to the mill
    Where Henry Clinton ground it.

Later the effigy was burnt.

The Pennsylvania Council felt uncomfortable with Peggy wandering loose in town. Before long, to quell rising commotion, the Council ordered Judge Shippen to escort his daughter out of state, into the arms of the British and her newly red-coated husband in New York City.

CHAPTER VIII

# Minority Report

*IN WHICH a sizable group of African-Americans fight for freedom on two levels at once in what can fairly be called the first battle of the Civil War.*

*IN 1775*, of a total population of two and a half million Americans, twenty-one percent, one out of every five, was African-American. Most of these were bound in slavery; only a handful were free citizens of the individual colonies. Thirty-eight percent of the slave population lived in Virginia, where two of every five Virginians were African-American. This compares to two of every forty Rhode Islanders, or two of every 100 persons in Massachusetts. Vermont, incidentally, never permitted slavery within its borders.

In his first draft of the Declaration of Independence, Thomas Jefferson—intellectually uncomfortable with the concept of involuntary servitude, though a slaveholder himself—excoriated George III as a cruel and despotic ruler who "determined to keep open a market where men should be bought and sold." But Jefferson's sentiment soon was knocked out of the final manifesto by both southern and northern Congressional delegates.

Under the initial devastating attacks of one of the world's most powerful standing armies, the Revolutionaries soon realized how foolish it was to limit Continental Army recruitment to whites only, ignoring the vast pool of African-American manpower on the North American continent. Besides acting as service troops, such recruits could also participate in the heavy fighting.

The number of African-Americans used by or in the army increased as the war went along. In addition to volunteer freemen, the substitute system prompted masters to send their slaves into the ranks in their place, or to bring them along, often with the promise of manumission at the war's end. Late in 1777, a Hessian officer en route to Boston with Burgoyne's surrendered army observed that "you never see a rebel regiment in which there are not some Negroes, well-built, strong, husky fellows."

At peak strength, therefore, the Continental Army averaged about fifty African-American soldiers to a batallion. One special adjutant general's return (24 August 1778) spoke of 755 Negroes on active duty with the Revolutionary army, with forty percent of these evenly divided between the New England and Virginia brigades.

Against this backdrop, the Revolution can be viewed as a missed opportunity for improved American racial relations, or alternatively, as the first battle of the Civil War.

*LIKE HALLEY'S COMET,* historic fact can be easily forgotten when it disappears from view. But, like the comet, it always reappears. For example, thirty-five years ago one of our better known historian-editors wrote what everyone thought would be the definitive book on the Battle of Bunker Hill. "The sluices, both of the blood of free men and of slaves," reminisced Deborah Gannett in 1802, "were first opened here." But the modern text somehow neglects to mention the significant participation in the battle by at least two African-Americans. One, Peter Salem, was a slave and a crack shot; the other, Salem Poor, was a leading Boston freeman.

The cause of black equality in the United States has never suffered from a lack of articulate white pleaders. On the Fourth of July 1847, a decade and a half before the Civil War, America's poet laureate John Greenleaf Whittier editorialized in the *National Era* on "The Black Men of the Revolution." Whittier observed:

> The return of our Festival of National Independence calls attention to a matter that has been very carefully kept out of sight by orators and toast-drinkers. I refer to the participation by colored men in the great struggle for Freedom.

It has not been so long since John Trumbull, artistic chronicler of major engagements of the Revolutionary War, acknowledged in his huge canvas "The Battle of Bunker Hill" the supportive role played by Peter Salem. Among the seventeen recognizable American and British participants in the battle that he portrays, Trumbull includes 2nd Lieutenant Thomas Grosvenor of the 3rd Connecticut Regiment and, directly behind him, his servant Peter Salem. During the battle, a shot from Salem's musket is credited with killing Major John Pitcairn, who two months earlier had been shooting down the dispersing Minute Men on Lexington green. Yet only a half-century later, as Whittier noted, the speechmakers were already remembering to forget. By painting Peter Salem into his famous canvas, now hanging in the Yale University Art Gallery, Trumbull—who personally witnessed the battle from Roxbury across the harbor—made Salem immortal.

But John Trumbull's first sketch in 1783 for the Bunker Hill battle canvas contained no likeness of Peter Salem. The inclusion of Lieutenant Grosvenor's companion was an afterthought. Perhaps the symbolic significance of an enslaved American participating in a life-and-death struggle for freedom on a Boston hilltop grew on the painter; two years later, he completed another portrait depicting only Grosvenor and his African-American servant.

In 1975, to coincide with the Bicentennial, the United States Postal Service issued a ten-cent stamp honoring Salem Poor, another notable African-American soldier at Bunker Hill. A 17 December 1775 petition on Poor's behalf to the Massachusetts General Court (Legislature) from fourteen Continental officers had praised Poor's service in Colonel Frye's regiment, where he "behaved like an experienced officer, as well as an excellent soldier."For those who had never heard of Poor, the commemorative postage stamp carried an explanatory tab: "GALLANT SOLDIER—The conspicuously courageous actions of black foot soldier Salem Poor at the Battle of Bunker Hill on June 17, 1775 earned him citations for bravery and leadership ability."

BY THE WINTER of 1777-1778, Congressionally ordered state troop levies for the Continental Army had scraped the bottom of the manpower barrel. In Rhode Island, the only state that lost population (nine percent) during the Revolution, the proportion of adult white males in the army, compared to the state's population as a whole, was abnormally high. The long British occupation of Newport, beginning 26 December 1776, exacerbated the difficulties of local recruiting.

In February 1778, over the stubborn objections of a small group of Rhode Island slaveowners, Governor Nicholas Cooke and the legislature pushed through a law authorizing enlistment of freemen and slaves from among the state's population of approximately 350 eligible African-American males to be formed into an African-American regiment, the 1st Rhode Island, which was to be officered by whites.

Slaves in the unit were promised their freedom at war's end; their owners were offered compensation of $150 per recruit.[1] With the blessing of Rhode Island General James Varnum and Washington's tacit approval, General Nathanael Greene took the lead in helping organize the new 130-man regiment.[2]

This Rhode Island/African-American contribution to the war distinguished itself at the hotly contested 29 August 1778 engagements north of Newport, where they were cited by their commanding general John Sullivan for demonstrating "desperate valor in repelling three furious assaults" by the Hessian infantry. The British eventually withdrew to New York, and the 1st Rhode Island continued to serve until the end of the war as far south as Virginia. Its officers included forty-one-year-old Colonel Christopher Greene (Nathanael Greene's third cousin, who had come up from Valley Forge to take command), Colonel Jeremiah Olney, and Majors Ebenezer Flagg and Samuel Ward, Jr.[3]

Traveling west from Newport on 5 January 1781 to join the main army, the 1st Rhode Island was observed at a Connecticut ferry crossing. The Marquis François Jean de Chastellux, one of Rochambeau's major generals, wrote in his journal: "The majority of the

[1] This compares most favorably with the thirty-five-dollar death bonus paid to German princes for each of the 7,554 lost Hessian mercenaries.

[2] Prescribed strength of a Rhode Island regiment in 1778 was 590 enlisted men. In practice, few of the customarily under-strength Continental Army regiments ever approached that number.

[3] Like Colonel Robert Shaw of the 54th Massachusetts Regiment during the Civil War, and "Black Jack" Pershing on the Mexican border in 1916, all 1st Rhode Island officers saw no discredit in training and leading African-American regular army troops.

enlisted men are Negroes or mulattoes. They are strong, robust men. Those I saw made a very good appearance."

On 15 April 1781, Greene's 1st Rhode Island was placed in a strong defensive position above the north bank of the Croton River, guarding that sector of the American lines that marked the northernmost portion of Westchester County's Neutral Ground. Those lines extended from the Van Cortlandt Manor House (where the Croton flows into the Hudson) along the north bank of the river toward Connecticut. The area covered by Greene's 1st Rhode Islanders included several fords across the Croton and one strategic bridge, Pine's Bridge. Pine's Bridge, over which the spy André, displaying Benedict Arnold's pass, had crossed the previous fall, was protected at all times. The guards at the river fords, however, were customarily withdrawn at sunrise on the assumption that the enemy would not attempt a daylight crossing of the Croton.

In the jargon of the time, the country around the river was "infested with Tories." Many others had fled to New York City to join Colonel James De Lancey's Westchester Refugee Corps. De Lancey, seeking an opportunity to strike an unexpected blow at the American positions, received word of the unguarded fords. Late on 13 May 1781 he assembled a force of sixty cavalry and 200 infantry, and moved north on back lanes across the Neutral Ground[4] towards the Croton River. Their destination remained his secret until Blenis Ford over the Croton River[5] was almost in sight. The expedition remained concealed in the woods on the south bank until the first gray light of 14 May, when the American guards were withdrawn for breakfast. De Lancey's troopers crashed out of the woods, galloped across the ford, and rode hell-for-leather up the steep hill towards the elegant Davenport home where Greene and his officers still lay sleeping.[6]

---

[4] The "Neutral Ground" in the American Revolution was that section of New York's Westchester County lying between the British and American battle lines.

[5] Two miles east of the site chosen fifty-five years later for the first Croton Aqueduct Dam.

[6] This was hardly the first British hit-and-run enemy cavalry attack in upper Westchester County, but it was one of the bloodiest. Two years before, on 2 July 1779, swashbuckling Lieutenant Colonel Banastre Tarleton had led his British Legion on a fiery raid against the villages of Bedford and Pound Ridge, inflicting

Angered by a pair of pistol shots from the house, De Lancey's Refugees dismounted and burst into the building, sabering Colonel Greene and killing Major Flagg and a junior officer. The enemy infantry quickly scattered the surprised Rhode Islanders, killing fourteen, wounding ten, and capturing thirty. De Lancey, without a single casualty, left as quickly as he had come, riding down the hill and crossing Pine's Bridge. The dying Colonel Greene, still in night-clothes, was tossed over a saddle, in which position he soon expired. His mangled body was uncermoniously dumped into a ditch, where it was discovered by pursuing American cavalry.

The shattered African-American Rhode Island Continentals were reconstituted under Colonel Olney and Major Ward.[7] Soon, convoying the artillery and baggage train, the 1st Rhode Island joined the great 5,982-man French-American march south to Virginia. At Cornwallis's surrender, these African-American freemen and soon-to-be-freemen stood alongside other Continental regiments from Maryland, Virginia, North and South Carolina, and Georgia, and acknowledged the salute of an enemy who had so recently almost destroyed them.

Keenly aware that their two-tiered struggle for liberty was unique among the Revolutionaries, the men of the 1st Rhode Island gave particular attention to their appearance and military discipline. Watching the Continental Army units pass in review before Washington and Rochambeau, Baron Ludwig von Closen, aide-de-camp to the French commander, noted in his journal that the 1st Rhode Islanders were the "most neatly dressed, the best under arms, and the most precise in their maneuvers."

---

twenty-one casualties and taking twenty prisoners. Such raids continued intermittently, occasionally matched by American forays in the opposite direction. "Bloody" Tarleton, stocky little redheaded son of a Lord Mayor of Liverpool, rose through the ranks, and at twenty-five was one of the youngest senior officers in the British Army. Boastful, dashing, and successful, he carried everything before him, until his cavalry unit was decisively defeated at the Battle of Cowpens, South Carolina. There, for the first time, Tarleton was forced to flee the field. His legendary brutal treatment of surrendering Americans gave rise to the phrase, "Tarleton's quarter," which was no quarter at all.

[7] The American dead, white officers and African-American rank and file, are interred beneath two separated stone memorials alongside the Crompond Presbyterian Church of Yorktown, on NY Route 202 east of the Taconic Parkway.

# CHAPTER IX

# Skinners----Friends or Foes?

*IN WHICH America's first novelist, seeking a juicier story line, casually confuses the good guys with the bad guys.*

*IT SHOULD NEVER* be too late to correct a libel, even though, as Mark Twain once joked, a lie is halfway around the world before the truth can pull up its pants. The patriot irregulars and militia who, during the Revolution, fought back and forth over the Neutral Ground against its British and German invaders have been, for more than a century and a half, sorely libeled. Ignoring printed evidence aged in the wood, so to speak, for more than 170 years, many popular authors and reputable historians have automatically accused these Neutral Ground American citizen-soldiers of war crimes equal to or worse than those actually committed by the British Army, its tory allies, and its German mercenaries. The dogged persistance of the libel merely shows how easily historical error can be perpetuated. To set the record straight, I believe the answer to the question in this chapter's title should be "Foes"—tory foes.

*FIRST DOCUMENTING*, and then undoing, what I consider to be a major error in our country's historical record is no easy task. To begin, I refer to Merriam-Webster's Unabridged *Third New International Dictionary of the English Language,*[1] for the following definition:

[1] Springfield, MA, 1968.

*Skinner:* one of a band of guerillas and irregular cavalry claiming attachment to either the British or American troops and operating in Westchester County in New York during the American Revolution.

Were the Skinners British or American? The entry is ambiguous. It also ignores the significant origin of the term. A "skinner" did not refer to a Revolutionary guerilla who "skinned" Hudson Valley farmers of their food, clothing, or household goods, as some believe; rather, a "Skinner" referred to a member of one of three battalions[2] of tory refugee volunteers raised by fifty-one-year-old erstwhile New Jersey Attorney General, British Brigadier General Cortlandt Skinner. Under his leadership, Skinner's Skinners saw partisan service for King George III in and around New York City from 1778 to the end of the war. They were one of two such loyalist corps and were nicknamed after their commanding general.

The other nickname, "Cowboys" was applied by Continental soldiers, militia, and patriot farmers to the provincial Westchester Light Horse Battalion, the tory corps raised a year earlier by Colonel James De Lancey. Distinctively uniformed in green jackets, the Light Horse cavalry were stationed in the Morrisania section of lower Westchester, near King's Bridge. The Cowboys raided regularly between the lines, rounding up food—especially beef cattle on the hoof; hence their sobriquet—for the British army and civilian population in lower Manhattan.

With one exception, a diary entry referred to below, a reader can find no mention of the supposedly ubiquitous Skinners of the Neutral Ground anywhere in the vast body of Revolutionary daybooks, journals, orders, and dispatches. On the other hand, references to De Lancey's Cowboys abound.

For example, in Joseph Plumb Martin's memoirs, Martin relates how an officer along the Hudson "had collected some stores of flour, port &c. for the use of the militia in his neighborhood. A party of the enemy denominated 'Cowboys' (Refugees) destroyed his stores." There is no mention whatever in Martin's work of Skinners—just Cowboys. But when a contemporary historian recently re-edited Martin's little book under the title, *Private Yankee Doodle*,[3] he found

---

[2] In the contending armies, the designations "battalion" and "regiment" were essentially interchangeable.

[3] Boston, 1962.

it necessary to add this footnote supplying what he considered important missing information: "The Tory sympathizers called themselves 'Cowboys' or 'Refugees,' and the rebel sympathizers called themselves 'Skinners.' " Private Martin might have been surprised.

HOW AND WHERE did this myth about Skinners arise? I suggest that it could only have come from the imaginations of James Fenimore Cooper and Washington Irving, those wonderful spinners of tales of fearless Americans in the Hudson Valley who conquered adversity, fell asleep for twenty years, and rode around with pumpkins perched on their heads. Early in their careers, both authors had sunk their teeth into the wartime history of the Valley, particularly Westchester County.

Cooper was born in Burlington, New Jersey, six years after the end of the Revolution. While still a child, he moved with his family to upstate New York, near the lake where General James Clinton assembled his troops and boats for the punitive expedition against the Iroquois in 1779 (see Chapter XI). Literary legend tells how, on an evening in 1820, Cooper tossed into the fire an English novel he was reading aloud to his wife, the former Susan De Lancey, a direct descendant of the militant tory family that included Colonel James De Lancey, commander of the Cowboys. "I could write a better story myself," claimed the thirty-year-old Cooper, a former naval officer. And he proceeded to make the attempt.

His first effort was a novel, Precaution, soon forgotten on both sides of the Atlantic. The Encyclopedia Britannica says of his next novel, The Spy: A Tale of the Neutral Ground, published anonymously in Philadelphia in 1821: "Never was a work written with such contemptuous carelessness." Despite only rare flashes of dramatic narrative buried beneath endless expository verbiage, The Spy still commanded three printings in its first year and quickly became the most successful novel yet published in the infant United States. It was unusual among the novels of the time for dealing with thinly disguised real persons and events. Cooper's Revolutionary subject matter possessed nostalgic appeal and also proved to be of great interest overseas, where this country was still largely geographic and political terra incognita. Cooper's mannered, prolix prose possibly may have improved in its many translations, including Russian.

In a special introduction, written long after *The Spy's* first publication, Cooper tells how its convoluted plot was derived principally from tales and anecdotes told to him by an anonymous Mr. __, now known to be his aging Westchester neighbor John Jay. It is interesting that the word "Skinner" is not to be found in any of Jay's public or private papers.

Jay, who also appears in Cooper's novel as Mr. Harper, was a key member of the Secret Committee of the New York State Convention that controlled Hudson Valley espionage during the Revolution. It was Jay who employed Enoch Crosby, the daring agent Cooper fictionalized as Harvey Birch, the country peddler and the spy referred to in the novel's title.

With a bow towards his wife's forebears, Cooper inserted a footnote in Chapter XVIII of *The Spy* asserting that Colonel James De Lancey's documented wartime cruelty was only "fancied. . .there is no evidence of his being guilty of any acts unusual in this species of warfare."[4]

Cooper's literary problem was that his imaginary British and American officers were always patrician gentlemen and unblemished heroes, while a counterbalance of villains to make a good wartime story was in short supply. Cooper's solution was to reach out and arbitrarily introduce the noun "Skinners" as an evil synonym for the American revolutionary irregulars.[5]

The word "Skinner" first appears on the final page of Chapter I of *The Spy*, as part of the incoherent utterances of the faithful old African-American retainer Caesar: "I been to see—Massa Harper on he knee—pray to God—no gemman who pray to God tell of good son come to see old fader—*Skinner* [emphasis added] do that—no Christian!" In the four paragraphs that follow and end the chapter, Cooper explains the reference:

[4] A century later, Otto Huefland's authoritative study, *Westchester County During the American Revolution*, supplied abundant evidence of some of De Lancey's "fancied" acts: "Abuse of women. . .clubbing and stabbing, repeated hanging up until nearly dead. . .applying hot coals to the soles of feet. . .tearing the seat from a chair, placing the naked victim on it, then kindling a fire under the chair."

[5] Mark Twain once accused Cooper of committing eighteen literary offenses in a single chapter. This, as it belies history, is yet another.

The convenience, and perhaps the necessities, of the leaders of the American arms, in the neighborhood of New York, had induced them to employ certain subordinate agents, of extremely irregular habits, in executing their lesser plans of annoying the enemy. It was not a moment for fastidious inquiries into abuses of any description, and oppression and injustice were the natural consequences of the possession of a military power that was uncurbed by the restraints of civil authority. In time, a distinct order of the community was formed, whose sole occupation appears to have been that of relieving their fellow citizens from any little excess of temporal prosperity they might be thought to enjoy, under the pretense of patriotism and the love of liberty.

Occasionally, the aid of military authority was not wanting, in enforcing these arbitrary distributions of worldly goods: and a petty holder of a commission in the state militia was to be seen giving the sanction of something like legality to acts of the most unlicensed robbery, and, not infrequently, of bloodshed.

On the part of the British, the stimulus of loyalty was by no means suffered to sleep, where so fruitful a field offered on which it might be expanded. But their freebooters were enrolled, and their efforts more systematized. Long experience had taught their leaders the efficacy of concentrated force; and, unless tradition does great injustice to their exploits, the result did no little credit to their foresight. The corps—we presume, from known affection to that useful animal—had received the quaint appellation of *Cowboys* [emphasis added].

Caesar was, however, far too loyal to associate men who held the commission of George III with the irregular warriors, whose excesses he had so often witnessed, and from whose rapacity neither his poverty nor his bondage had suffered even him to escape uninjured. The Cowboys, therefore, did not receive their proper portion of the black's censure, when he said, no Christian, nothing but a Skinner, could betray a pious child, while honoring his father with a visit so full of peril.

Cooper thus moved to establish villains to match his heroes, thereby creating a false myth about the Skinners, who continue to wander in and out of the novel's remaining 170,000 words. The story ends with the death of the spy Harvey Birch on a Canadian battlefield—in the War of 1812!

In Chapter X, Cooper describes the leader of the Skinners:

A man still young in years, but his lineaments bespoke a mind long agitated by evil passions. His dress was of the meanest materials, and so ragged and unseemly, as to give him the appearance of studied poverty. His hair was prematurely whitened, and his sunken, lowering eye avoided the bold forward look of innocence. There was a restlessness in his manner, that proceeded from the workings of the foul spirit within him, and which was not less offensive to others than distressing to himself. This man was a well known leader of one of these gangs of marauders who infested the county with a semblance of patriotism, and who were guilty of every grade of offense, from simple theft to murder.

Cooper, having thus established the imaginary character of his Westchester County irregulars, then has, in Chapter XIV, a Skinner raiding party burn Birch's house. A troop of respectable Virginia cavalry horsewhips the Skinners in Chapter XVIII. The Skinners burn another home in Chapter XXII. And in Chapter XXXII, in one of the grimmest scenes in American literature, the turncoat Skinner leader is lynched by two Cowboy officers, but not before crying out: "Help! Cut the rope!—Birch! good peddler! Down with the Congress!—Sergeant! For God's sake, help! Hurrah for the King!—O God—mercy, mercy—mercy!"

When Cooper published *The Spy* in 1821, no aging British military refugee volunteers came forward to comment on the author's application of a tory military nickname to a fictional group of patriotic bandits. It was, after all, four decades after the Revolution, and most members of General Skinner's corps had long since gone to their reward after being evacuated to England or Nova Scotia. But a corrective to Cooper's description of Skinners appeared almost immediately in the published memoirs of Continental Army surgeon James Thacher.

Dr. Thacher was not only a trained medical man, but also an astute historical observer and diarist. Born in 1754, he lived for ninety years, serving the Revolution from the siege of Boston to the surrender at Yorktown. In his sixty-ninth year, Thacher published his two-volume *Military Journal During The American Revolutionary War, From 1775 to 1783, Describing Interesting Events and Transactions of This Period, with Numerous Historical Facts and Anecdotes.*[6]

In *The Spy*, Cooper's compassionate Continental Army dragoon surgeon-philosopher, Dr. Archibald Sitgreaves, appears to have been modeled on the talented Dr. Thacher. "It was a maxim with Dr. Sitgreaves," wrote Cooper, "that no species of knowledge was to be despised."

Thacher's memoirs, drawn from his wartime diary, recall his long service in the American Revolution. In the fall of 1780, he was stationed in the lower Hudson Valley. His journal entry for 24 November reads:

> The country which we lately traversed, about 50 miles in extent, is called neutral ground, but the miserable inhabitants who remain are not much favored with the privileges which their neutrality ought to secure to them. They are continually exposed to the ravages and insults of infamous banditti, composed of royal refugees and tories. The country is rich and fertile, and the farms appear to have been advantageously cultivated, but it now has the marks of a country in ruins. A large proportion having abandoned their farms, the few that remain find it impossible to harvest the produce. The meadows and pastures are covered with grass of a summer's growth, and thousands of bushels of apples and other fruit are rotting in the orchard. We brought off about two hundred loads of hay and grain, and ten times the amount might have been procured, if teams enough had been provided. Those of the inhabitants of the neutral ground who were Tories, have joined their friends in New York, and the Whigs have retired into the interior of our country. *Some of each side* [emphasis added] have taken up arms, and become the most cruel and deadly foes. There are— within the British lines—*banditti* [emphasis added] consisting of lawless villains, who devote themselves to the most cruel pillage and robbery among the defenceless inhabitants between the lines, many of whom they carry off to New York, after plundering their houses and farms. These shameless marauders have received the names of *Cow-boys and Skinners* [emphases added]. By their atrocious deeds they have become a scourge and terror to the people.

Thacher's story is straightforward. It is quoted at length here because his diary contains the sole firsthand reference to Skinners in any form that survives today from the American Revolution. Every-

---

[6] Boston, 1823. The *Military Journal* was only part of Thacher's prolific output. He also wrote an *American Medical Biography*, *The American Orchardist*, *The Management of Bees*, *Demonology, Ghosts, and Apparitions*, and a *History of the Town of Plymouth*.

thing else is later and secondhand. Even the most casual reading of Thacher's entry reveals that the antecedent of his nouns, "These shameless marauders...*Cow-boys and Skinners*," is not "Some of each side," but "*banditti*...within the British lines." Skinners were British banditti, never Americans. After 1823, only the most inattentive historical reader could support a contrary view.

But why did Cooper slip so easily into his characterization of Westchester's angry and impoverished patriot yeomen, ascribing to them the frightful depredations of their opponents, Skinner's tory volunteers? After all, two generations had passed since the Revolution, and printed descriptions of British devastation in the area were not uncommon. Chaplain Timothy Dwight's haunting panorama of the Boston Post Road from New Rochelle to Rye during that period of the Revolution is only one example:

> Where I had heretofore seen a continual succession of horses and carriages, and life and bustle lent a sprightliness to all the environ-ing objects, not a single, solitary traveler was visible from week to week, or from month to month.[7]

In 1821, when Cooper wrote his novel, the United States was still slowly working its way towards what would soon be known as "Jacksonian democracy," through the Embargo Act of 1807, the 1814 separatist Hartford Convention, and the Panic (and first Immigration Law) of 1819. Disturbing memories of Shays's violent 1787 agrarian revolt in Massachusetts, Pennsylvania's equally tumultuous 1794 Whiskey Rebellion, and Fries's 1799 Uprising still lingered with literate, propertied Americans. This group included most of Cooper's readers. Cooper, the eleventh of twelve children from an early log cabin family, had successfully married into this stratum of society. To many of his audience, the concept of a class of terrifying, quasi-patriotic Westchester Skinners was perfectly acceptable.

Beginning with Cooper's literary invention and continuing until the present day, a parade of more than three dozen fiction writers, historians, and encyclopedists appears to have absorbed *The Spy's* characterization of marauding Revolutionaries, and thus innocently perpetuated the "patriot Skinner" myth.

[7] Timothy Dwight, *Travels in New-England and New-York.* (New Haven, 1821). Dwight had become president of Yale College.

Grand Marshal of this parade has been that other wonderful
spinner of tall tales, Washington Irving. He added fresh life to
Cooper's misidentification in *A Chronicle of Wolfert's Roost*:

> Hence arose those two great orders of border chivalry, the Skinners
> and the Cow-boys, famous in the heroic annals of Westchester
> County. The former fought, or rather marauded, under the Ameri-
> can, the latter under the British banner; but both, in the hurry of
> their military ardor, were apt to err on the safe side, and rob friend
> as well as foe. Neither of them stopped to ask the politics of a horse
> or cow, which they drove into captivity; nor, when they wrung
> the neck of a rooster, did they trouble their heads to ascertain
> whether he were crowing for Congress or King George.

Here is a disturbing demonstration of how easily anecdotal and
inaccurate information can be disseminated as truth. It is dismaying
how many other thoughtful and distinguished historical writers and
researchers during the last century and a half have picked up and even
embroidered the whole cloth of Cooper's allegations about the
Skinners.

First in line after Irving was the historian Jared Sparks, who
served four years as chaplain of the House of Representatives and
later became president of Harvard College. His biography of Benedict
Arnold asserts:

> The Skinners and Cow-Boys often leagued together. The former
> would sell their plunder to the latter, taking in exchange contra-
> band articles brought from New York. It was not uncommon for
> the farce of a skirmish to be acted near the American lines, in which
> the Skinners never failed to come off victorious; and then they
> would go boldly to the interior with their booty, pretending it had
> been captured from the enemy while attempting to smuggle it
> across the lines.[8]

Robert P. Bolton's *History of the County of Westchester* adds flavor
to Cooper's myth:

> There was another description of banditti, called 'Skinners,' who
> lived, for the most part, within the American lines, and professed

[8] Boston, 1834.

attachment to the American cause; but, in reality, they were more unprincipled, perfidious and inhuman than the Cowboys themselves; for these latter exhibited some symptoms of fellow feeling for their friends,—whereas, the Skinners committed their depredations equally upon friends and foes.[9]

Occasionally a warning flag went up, to which nobody paid much attention. For example, in 1854, John M. McDonald delivered several papers before members of the New-York Historical Society under the general title, *The Neutral Ground of Westchester*. The work was based on a total of 407 interviews with 241 different County residents born before the Revolution. Only one of McDonald's aged interviewees, a man of 84, made any mention of "Skinners"—and he confused their activities with those of the cattle-rustling cowboys.

Ignoring the implications of these firsthand McDonald interviews, Benson J. Lossing's *Pictorial Field Book of the American Revolution* further enriches the Skinner myth:

The Skinners generally professed attachments to the American cause, and lived chiefly within the patriot lines; but they were of easy virtue. . .treacherous, rapacious, and often brutal.[10] Lossing also repeated Sparks's twenty-six-year-old depiction.

Moving into the present century, Lossing, now editing the "Encyclopedia of United States History," inserts a Skinner entry: "A predatory band in the Revolutionary War whose members professed to be Whigs. They were not very scrupulous in their choice of victims, plunder being their chief aim."[11]

Scribners' authoritative "Dictionary of American History" uses "ironically" to iron out the ambiguity of its entry: "The Skinners, ironically named after Gen. Cortlandt Skinner's Brigade of New Jersey volunteers. . .claimed attachment sometimes to the British and sometimes to the Americans."[12]

[9] New York, 1848.

[10] New York, 1860.

[11] New York and London, 1902.

[12] New York, 1940.

In 1958, Allison Albee, writing in the Westchester Historical Society's *Westchester Historian*, made an assertion that goes far beyond anything even Cooper invented: "The Patriot Skinners worked under arrangement with the regular Continental Army command."[13]

James H. Pickering followed up a decade later in the same magazine: "The Skinners seem to have been an anomalous group . . .what turned a 'patriot' into a 'Skinner' apparently, was the failure to discriminate between friend and foe."[14]

In *The Price of Loyalty*, Catherine S. Crary leveled the strongest allegation to date of rapacity and cruelty: "The rebel counterpart of the Cowboys were the Skinners, so-called because they robbed and often murdered their victims. They were banditti. . .some of whom were simply bent on depredation and gainful plunder under the sinister guise of patriotism. . .committing inhuman acts of banditry on hapless Westchester farmers whenever convenient.[15] Crary followed her denunciation with a lengthy quotation from Thomas Jones's *History of New York During the Revolutionary War*[16] published by The New-York Historical Society, which she captions: "The Skinners Plunder and Burn the Seat of General Oliver De Lancey and Treat the Ladies of His Family Barbarously." But nowhere in Jones's own writing does the word "Skinner" appear.

Again, in the 1975 *Loyalist Americans*, a collection of essays edited by historians Robert A. East and Jacob Judd, Crary considers British guerilla activities in Westchester under the subtitle, "Conventional Warfare or Self-Interested Freebooting?" and follows the same line as Cooper's *Spy*. She uses the American experience in Vietnam as an analogy to illustrate the "hazy bounds of conventional warfare," and concludes that "the opprobrium heaped on [the Cowboys] at the end of the war went to extremes, and was not justified."

At the same time, curiously enough, her position on the Skinners softened: "Skinners, their rebel counterpart, skinned their victims of purses and clothes; the Skinners in general supported the rebels."[17]

---

[13] White Plains, 1958.

[14] White Plains, 1967.

[15] New York, 1973.

[16] New York, 1979. (Edward Floyd De Lancey, ed.)

[17] Crary: "Guerilla Activities of James De Lancey's Cowboys in Westchester County." Tarrytown, 1975.

Crary also repeats Pickering's 1967 comment from *The Westchester Historian.*

Even so thoroughly researched a work as Mark Mayo Boatner III's *Encyclopedia of the American Revolution*[18] equivocates: "The Cowboys were generally concluded to be Tories and the Skinners patriots."

In a 1987 novel about Major André by the British author Anthony Bailey, André "reminisces" after his capture:

> The militia Captain had warned us about Skinners, the rebel volunteers who served the Continental cause by. . .terrorizing the Westchester countryside. . .some of them moving back and forth, serving both armies as it suited their own interests.

Putting all such questionable scholarship behind us, one nagging thought remains: Had James Fenimore Cooper not married into the De Lancey family, would the Revolutionary irregulars of Westchester County have gone down in history, not as cutthroat Skinners, but as true patriots, even as effective, selfless, and dedicated as old Leatherstocking himself?

When will Cooper's literary invention finally lose its hold on history? Early in the 20th century, an American behavorial psychologist invented a famous little box with slides and doors that condition the reflexes of thousands of hungry rats and pigeons. Its message was simple: "Do it the traditional way and you'll be fed." His last name, curiously enough, was Skinner.

[18] New York, 1975.

CHAPTER X

# Death of a Nation

*IN WHICH Sachem Daniel Nimham and his dispossessed Wappingers express the last full measure of their devotion to the new republic.*

*IN THE LATE* summer of 1776, as Washington prepared to defend New York City against enemy invasion, most adult males of the Wappinger nation at Stockbridge, Massachusetts, led by their Sachem Daniel Nimham, marched to the Upper Hudson Valley to join the Northern Department campaign. The American defense in that theatre of war, commanded by Major General Philip Schuyler, teetered at the edge of disaster. Thousands of British troops under the competent command of Sir Guy Carleton had gathered below Montreal, ready to strike south along Lake Champlain towards Albany. After overrunning the retreating Americans, Carelton planned to join with General Sir William Howe, who was expected to move up the Hudson River from New York City.

A single obstacle blocked Carleton's advance. Hastily launched by Benedict Arnold (before his treason) from an improvised dockyard at the south end of Lake Champlain, a tiny flotilla of armed schooners, gondolas, and row galleys was poised to strike defensively up and down the lake at Carleton's supply lines.

The British leader was forced to pause at St. John's, fretfully watching the critical summer months of 1776 slip away while he constructed his own fleet.

On 4 October, Carleton's eighty-seven-gun flotilla finally set sail down the lake towards Fort Ticonderoga, while his army of British Regulars and German mercenaries (hired by the King without Parliamentary approval, and eventually adding up to a third of the royal forces in North America) marched four abreast down the western shore. Racing ahead of his ground troops, Carleton's fifty-three-vessel naval force cornered Arnold's undermanned, outgunned vessels behind Valcour Island on 11 October.

After a brutal action, the survivors among the 820 Revolutionary soldiers-turned-sailors were able to steal away by night under cover of a fortuitous fog. The Americans landed at Crown Point and, after some heavy skirmishing, marched eight miles to rejoin the 6,000-man garrison at Fort Ticonderoga—where Arnold promptly squabbled over command.

But he had accomplished his purpose. It was now too late in the year for Carleton to invest Ticonderoga, the most powerful fortification in North America. On 3 November, the British commander drew back from Crown Point to winter quarters at St. John's. The enemy's 1776 campaign to cut the Revolution in half along the line of the Hudson Valley was postponed until spring.

*IN JUNE 1777*, with Lake Champlain free of winter ice, the invasion of New York State was launched under a new commander, General John Burgoyne. We have seen in *Chapter VI* how this brought Obadiah Brown back into battle as part of a powerful force of militia and Continentals that also included Daniel Nimham's Stockbridge Wappingers.

Stationed between Forts Ann and Edward under General John Nixon, Nimham, his two sons, Aaron and John, and the other Wappinger warriors helped harass Burgoyne's rear guard. On 18 July, with four other scouts, Nimham reconnoitered Skenesborough[1] and returned the following day with two British Regulars and four tories as prisoners.

Nimham reported to General Nixon:

We passed the creek and went within a mile or two of Skene's house,[2] where we lay down in thick woods by the side of the road. It was not too long before there came along two regulars, driving a number of horses. We jumped up and seized them. The regulars

---

[1] Soon renamed Whitehall, New York.

[2] Major Philip Skene was an influential local tory. In 1776, Arnold used the sawmill at Skenesborough to construct his fleet.

were so very much frightened, they made no resistance; neither could they speak plain.

We found there were a number more behind, driving cattle, and one of our prisoners called to their sergeant for help; upon this we thought it wise to make the best way out of the woods. Our prisoners attempted to get away from us; we were obliged to make them feel our hatchets very heavy. I told them, "If you will behave like prisoners, we will use you well. If you don't, we must kill you." After this, they behaved well and did everything we bid them.

On our way back to our encampment, we thought we would take in as many Tories as we could find. In order to find them out, we gave our prisoners back their guns, taking out the flints. We came to a house and we told our prisoners, "You must keep before us, and if you see any man, you must cock your guns and present them at them, and demand who they are for: King or Country?"

They did so, and the Tories answered they were for the King, or they would have moved off long ago. They seemed glad to see the regulars, and told them, "You are our brothers." I knew one of the Tories, therefore as I came in sight of him, I put my hat over my face till the Redcoats had done their duty, for fear the fellow should know me.

After he had in a most strong manner declared he was for the King, I asked him, "Will you be true to the King, and fight for him till you die?" "Oh, yes," said the Tory. Upon this, he discovered his error, knew me, and immediately said, "What king do you mean?" "I mean King Hancock." "Ah," said I, "we have found you out. We don't know Kings in America now. You must go along with us."

THIS INCIDENT of Schuyler's delaying action in the woods above Fort Edward took place during his final days as commander of the Northern Department. On 4 August, a nervous Congress voted to replace him with his fractious subordinate, Horatio Gates. Gates prayed for time. It was nearing the end of summer; if he could fend off Burgoyne for only a few additional weeks, the ranks of his 3,000 Continentals could be augmented by four times that number of militia, who by then would have completed their essential harvesting chores.

Stumbling through the woods between Forts Ann and Edward, the British army developed serious problems with supplies. As we have seen, Burgoyne detached almost a fifth of his troops, mainly

German mercenaries, southeastward in search of forage and fresh mounts. Obadiah Brown was among the American militiamen under General John Stark, backed by a handful of Continental soldiers, who confronted the enemy at Bennington on 16 August. Burgoyne's entire campaign was now unhinged.

One month later, after a series of large- and small-scale engagements[3] on rolling fields above the west bank of the Hudson at Saratoga, Burgoyne surrendered his entire remaining 5,700 men to General Gates's. Most of Gates's jubilant militiamen went home, not to fight again in the Revolution. But they had been in the right place at the right time and had done their job well. Howe still had not returned from Philadelphia to fulfill his role in the grand strategy. "Philadelphia had captured Howe," the wags said. Sir Henry Clinton in New York made only a halfhearted effort to come up the Hudson to Burgoyne's support. The looming threat of invasion from the north had been smashed. Washington could now fight a simpler war.

The American victory at Saratoga on 17 October, and the subsequent formal French Alliance it underwrote, converted British military strategy against the United States into a giant punitive holding action. The Crown was now battling massive French, Spanish, and Dutch sea and land forces in the West Indies, India, Gibraltar, the Mediterranean, and along the Channel coast. Still ahead for the Americans lay the terrible winter of 1777-78 at Valley Forge, an unparalleled trial for the Continental troops, while Howe and his army lay nearby in the comfort of the usurped Revolutionary capital.

PROTECTING THE British lines around Philadelphia was a detachment of 494 mixed light troops, accompanied by fifty camp women, drawn from eleven companies originally raised by Colonel Robert Rogers from loyalists living in the New York City area. These "Queen's Rangers," who had sailed with Howe to the Chesapeake the previous September, distinguished themselves in the cat-and-mouse maneuvering and capture of Philadelphia that followed.

On 15 October, Howe assigned to the Rangers a new commander, the thirty-six-year-old Major John Graves Simcoe, who was shifted from the Grenadiers and advanced in rank from captain. In

---

[3] Including the Wappingers' bloodless capture 1 October of a British foraging party digging potatoes.

his *Military Journal*, Major Simcoe describes his new command of exclusively Provincial troops in these glowing terms:

> Young men, active, full of love of service, emulous to distinguish themselves in it, looking forward to obtain, through their actions, the honor of being enrolled with the main British Army. They were men already exiled for their attachment to the British government, and who now acted upon the firmest principles in its defense. They never considered the people they had to oppose as engaged in an honorable cause, or fighting for freedom of country.[4]
>
> They estimated them not by their words but by an intimate observance of their actions; and to civil desecration, experience had taught them to add military contempt.

Simcoe was a self-important young martinet, consistently seeking dangerous and unusual military assignments. Partisan warfare, he felt, not only "gave one the opportunity for self-dependence and prompt decisions," but also offered the "best mode of instruction for those who aim at higher station." As a young officer during the siege of Boston, he had approached Admiral Thomas Graves with an (ignored) plan to enlist a body of local African-Americans to strike against Rhode Island. Three years later in Philadelphia, he proposed to his commander that the Rangers be detached to the upper Delaware River to cooperate with Captain Walter Butler and his Iroquois allies. Simcoe's superiors "much applauded his spirit, but found sufficient employment for him with the present army."

Whereupon the young British commander set about to remold the Rangers in his image. He altered their headgear and uniforms to make them less conspicuous while on patrol. He abolished sergeant's guards and insisted on regularity in meals. Excessive written orders were discouraged; officers and men were encouraged to become self-reliant in the field, dispersing and regrouping with rapidity.

---

[4] Less than a decade after the Revolution, Simcoe was made the first Governor General of Canada. The Duke de la Rochefoucault-Liancourt, traveling at that time through North America, noted Simcoe's continuing "inveterate hatred against the United States." The Governor General himself wrote in 1792, "There is no person, perhaps, who thinks less of the talents and integrity of Mr. Washington than I do."

Marching was always at a quick pace. The Rangers were drilled to use their bayonets with force and effect, to fire with precision and steadiness. Simcoe was actually pointing his command towards the 19th century.

He was a formidable opponent to the Continentals, particularly to those who lay freezing twenty miles away at Valley Forge. Only the worst winter in memory kept the two groups apart.

Fallout from Burgoyne's disaster prompted an order from the King and Cabinet on 21 March 1778 to replace General William Howe in Philadelphia with General Sir Henry Clinton, and to pull back the British army of occupation overland to New York. The troopships that had carried the men down to Chesapeake Bay the previous summer were now urgently needed elsewhere in the world. It was high time to reunite the remaining British forces in North America; a French fleet was reliably reported en route from Brest.

The new commander advanced the energetic Simcoe to the rank of Lieutenant Colonel; his Rangers were deployed as a rearguard cavalry patrol on 18 June, when Clinton's 15,000-man army started out across New Jersey for New York. Simcoe fought off groups of pursuing Continentals under Generals von Steuben and Lafayette. In the 28 June Battle of Monmouth (see *Chapter VII*), Clinton's indefatigable Ranger chief took a ball in his arm that immobilized him for several weeks.

Carried to New York to convalesce, Simcoe inserted the following advertisement in James Rivington's *New York Royal Gazette*:

ALL ASPIRING HEROES have now an opportunity of distinguishing themselves by joining THE QUEEN'S RANGER HUZZARS Commanded by LIEUTENANT-COLONEL SIMCOE. Any spirited young man will receive every encouragement, be immediately mounted on an elegant horse, and furnished with clothing, accoutrements, &c. to the amount of FORTY GUINEAS, by applying to Cornet Spencer, at his quarters at No. 103 Water Street. Whoever brings in a recruit shall instantly receive TWO GUINEAS. VIVANT REX ET REGINA.

*BEFORE THE RETURN* of the Rangers to the New York area, British lines north of Manhattan were patrolled by a corps of tory chasseurs under the command of mercenary Lieutenant Colonel Andreas Emmerich. (The previous year in Philadelphia, Emmerich had writ-

ten *An Deutschen in Amerika*, a passionate appeal to Americans of
German descent to rally round the British flag.) Emmerich's corps
consisted of two infantry companies—one armed with muskets, the
other with rifles—and a troop of light dragoons trained for rapid
maneuver. The foot and mounted soldiers were mostly young men,
natives of New York City or refugees from Westchester County,
Dutchess County, or western Connecticut.

Colonel Emmerich had been born in Hanover and educated as a
soldier. He had served in Germany during the Seven Years' War
(1756-63) at the head of a party of rangers. Simcoe notes:

> He was sent out to the assistance of royalty in this country with a
> reputation, said to have been justly deserved, of possessing extraor-
> dinary abilities as a partisan. During the first years of the war, his
> chasseurs became very celebrated, and did the Crown good service;
> but afterward, partly from the severity of his discipline and partly
> from his foreign birth and manners, his men became dissatisfied.
> Most of his officers sought service under other commanders.

Emmerich's fierce sallies at the American lines in lower
Westchester actually served Washington well. Wishing to avoid any
major engagement that might seriously compromise his numerically
inferior forces, the commander in chief was still willing to commit
small American patrols and scouting parties to raids and ambushes.
They nipped at the enemy defenses by the Harlem River near King's
Bridge, constantly threatening the British troops on Manhattan
Island. Serving among Washington's scouts during the summer of
1778 were the two companies of Stockbridge soldiers led by Daniel
Nimham, with the rank of captain.

With troops retrieved from Philadelphia, Sir Henry Clinton
acted quickly to strengthen his northern perimeter. He placed Emmerich's Chasseurs with the Queen's Rangers, all under the command of Simcoe. The British fortifications guarding the two upper
Harlem River bridge crossings consisted of a chain of redoubts laid
out on several small hills that overlooked the river and the surrounding countryside to the north and east.

Half a mile in front of these redoubts was the Rangers' encampment. Beyond it to the north, towards the main American positions,
lay an irregular wooded country, broken by stone walls well suited

for ambushes. It was peopled by farm families of mixed political sentiments, who had already suffered greatly from the incessant raids and guerilla warfare of the Neutral Ground.

Across these slowly deteriorating farmsteads, American and British patrols felt each other out, cautiously at first, then more aggressively. Another young British officer, Oxford educated Lieutenant Colonel Banastre Tarleton, joined Simcoe's group. In December 1776, Tarleton had helped capture dawdling General Charles Lee near Basking Ridge, New Jersey.

On 1 August 1778, the twenty-four-year-old officer was posted to command the Rangers' Cavalry Legion. In Tarleton, Simcoe found "a colleague full of enterprise and spirit, anxious for every opportunity to distinguish himself." Both men had not long to wait—as Simcoe was somewhat stiffly to report in his *Journal*:

> Patrolling with a few hussars, making observations on the country in front, they had a singular and narrow escape. A girl, from a garret window, had seen some of our soldiers on the march through the woods, and gave the enemy intelligence. The inhabitants, so harrassed by their country being the seat of war, were by no means to be trusted.
>
> The Stockbridge Indians, about 60 in number, excellent marksmen, had joined Mr. Washington's[5] Army. Lt. Col. Simcoe was describing a private road to Lt. Col. Tarleton. Wright, his orderly dragoon, alighted and took down a fence of Devoe's farmyard, for them to pass through; around this farm the Indians were ambuscaded. Wright had scarce mounted his horse when these officers, for some trivial reason, altered their intentions and spurring their horses, and soon rode out of sight and out of reach of the Indians.
>
> In a few days after, the officers had certain information of the ambuscade which they so fortunately had escaped. In all probability they owed their lives to the Indians' expectations of surrounding and taking them prisoners.

---

[5] Although Simcoe published his *Journal* four years after the Treaty of Paris that ended the Revolution, he still could not bring himself to accord General Washington his proper military title. The publication of the *Journal* in the United States in 1844 occasioned considerable attack on Simcoe's accuracy as a reporter; he was shown to have "twisted facts and oversimplified involved situations in order to make it appear that his Rangers were invulnerable and did not engage in ruthless warfare."

Nimham and his scouts through an ironic development, were now under the command of General John Morin Scott, headquartered at Eastchester. Scott was the attorney who defended the Philipse family against Nimham's 1767 legal action to recover his nation's purloined lands (see *Chapter II*).

It was a strategically touchy time around New York. In Newport, cooperating with seventeen French warships, seven thousand Continental soldiers were besieging an equal number of British troops. Washington hung on Clinton's reaction. Would the British general throw major support to General Robert Pigot's men in Rhode Island, perhaps even evacuate New York City? "I am very anxious to obtain a true account of what is passing in New York," wrote the commander in chief on 25 August. He even reactivated plans for an attack on Fort Washington,[6] to be followed by reoccupation of the city. On 28 August he added, "Whether the enemy mean to transfer the war elsewhere, or intend to embrace the present opportunity of evacuating the Continent, is as yet uncertain."

Seeking every possible scrap of information on British intentions, Washington ordered General Scott to intensify his patrols of outlying British positions. For his part, Simcoe continued his forays, with attempted ambushes of the now far-extended Americans, who were busily, "in their antiquated dialect," wrote Simcoe, "scouting."

*THEN, RELATES SIMCOE* on 29 August:

> . . .[R]eturning from headquarters, Lt. Col. Simcoe heard firing in front, and being informed that Lt. Col Emmerich had patrolled, he immediately marched to his assistance. He soon met him retreating, and Lt. Col. Emmerich being of the opinion the rebels were in such force that it would be advisable to retreat, he did so. Lt. Col. Simcoe understood that Nimham, an Indian chief, and some of his tribe, were with the enemy. By his spies, who were excellent, he was informed that the enemy were highly elated at the retreat of Emmerich's corps, and applied it to the whole of the light troops at Kingsbridge. Lt. Col. Simcoe took measures to increase their belief, and ordering a day's provision to be cooked, marched on the morning of the 31st of August[7] a small distance in

---

[6] Now named Fort Knyphausen to honor its 1776 conqueror.

[7] Two days earlier, north of Newport, Rhode Island, the 1st Rhode Island Regiment (see *Chapter VIII*) had beaten back General Pigot's Hessian troops.

front of the post, determined to wait there the whole day in the hopes of betraying the enemy into an ambuscade; the country was most favorable to it. His idea was, as the enemy moved upon the road[8] intersecting the country, to advance from his flanks. This movement would be perfectly concealed by the fall of ground upon his right[9] and by the woods upon the left,[10] and he meant to gain the heights[11] in the rear of the enemy, attacking whomsoever should be within, by his cavalry and such infantry as might be necessary.

But Emmerich created difficulties.

In pursuance of these intentions, Lt. Col. Emmerich with his corps was detached from the Queen's Rangers and Legion; as Lt. Col. Simcoe thought, fully instructed in the plan. However, he most unfortunately mistook the nearer house [Daniel Devoe] for one at a greater distance [Frederick Devoe on today's McLean Avenue], the names being the same, and there he posted himself, and soon after sent from thence a patrol forward upon the road, before Lt. Col. Simcoe could have time to stop it.

But Simcoe was lucky.

The patrol had no bad effect, not meeting with any enemy; had a single man of it deserted or been taken, the whole attempt had probably been aborted. Lt. Col. Simcoe, who was halfway up a tree on the top of which was a drummer boy, saw a flanking party of the enemy approach. The troops had scarcely fallen into their ranks when a smart firing was heard from the Indians, who had lined the fences of the road and were exchanging shot with Lt. Col. Emmerich, whom they had discovered.

One of Emmerich's lieutenants picks up the story:

At 12 o'clock, Lt. Col. Emmerich discovers a body of rebel infantry of between 50 and 60 Indians coming down the road directly for

[8] Now Kimball Avenue in Bronx County.

[9] The sloping west bank of the Bronx River.

[10] Now Woodlawn Cemetery and Van Cortlandt Park, since 1898, part of Greater New York City.

[11] Now Woodlawn Heights.

him. He immediately made an attack on them, and then kept retreating by degrees in order to draw them through the right and left wings; which as soon as he found accomplished by the warm firing of his Light Infantry and Riflemen, and the Grenadiers of the Rangers, he immediately faced about and ordered a charge of his own Dragoons, accompanied by those of the Legion.

Simcoe resumes the story:

The Queen's Rangers moved rapidly to gain the heights and Lt. Col. Tarleton immediately advanced with the Hussars and the Legion cavalry. Not being able to pass the fences in his front, he made a circuit to return further upon their right. Which being reported to Lt. Col. Simcoe, he broke from the column of the Rangers, and directing Major Ross to conduct the Corps to the heights, advanced to the road and arrived, without being perceived, within ten yards of the Indians.

They had been intent upon the attack of Emmerich's Corps and the Legion; they now gave a yell and fired upon the Grenadier company, wounding four of them and Lt. Col. Simcoe.

This advance party of Nimham and his soldiers, on foot, most with discharged muskets, none with bayonets, heavily outnumbered by mounted British and German cavalry, cut off from the remainder of the Continental patrol under Major John Stewart, fought as best they could.

They were driven from the fences and Lt. Col. Tarleton with the cavalry got among them, and pursued them rapidly down Cortlandt's Ridge. That active officer had a narrow escape; in striking at one of the fugitives, he lost his balance and fell from his horse. Luckily the Indian had no bayonet and his musket had been discharged.

The Indian turned, however, upon his assailant, who now lay stretched upon the ground, and whom he was about to dispatch with the butt-end of his firelock. At this moment, Murphy, a dragoon belonging to the Legion, galloped forward and saved his commander.

The Indians fought most gallantly; they pulled more than one of the cavalry from their horses. French, an active youth, bugle-horn to the Hussars, struck at an Indian but missed his blow. The man dragged him from his horse and was searching for his knife to

stab him, when, loosening French's hand, the bugler luckily drew
out a pocket pistol and shot the Indian through the head, in which
situation he was found. One of the Legion cavalry was killed, and
one of them, and two of the Hussars, wounded.[12] Lt. Col. Simcoe
joined the battalion and seized the heights. A captain of the rebel
infantry and a few of his men were taken, but a body of them under
Major Stewart, who afterwards was distinguished at Stony Point,[13]
left the Indians and fled.[14] Though this ambuscade in its greater part
failed, it was of consequence. Nearly 40 of the Indians were killed
or desperately wounded, among others Nimham, a chieftain, who
had been in England,[15] and his sons. And it was reported to have
stopped a larger number of them, who were excellent marksmen,
from joining Mr. Washington's army.

The Indian doctor [shaman] was taken, and he said that when
Nimham saw the Grenadiers close in his rear, he called out to his
people to fly, and 'that he himself was an old tree, and would die
there.'

He wounded Lt. Col. Simcoe and was killed by Wright, his
orderly hussar.

Forty-seven years later, one of the Devoe daughters recalled to
her grandson:

Several Indians escaped through the woods and swamps. Others
ran down the ridge and across a small bridge over Tibbett's Brook,
a half mile distant, where, on the other side, a few of them hid
among the rocks and bushes. The cavalry, being unable to scale the
rocks, called upon the fugitives to surrender, promising them life
and freedom as a condition for so doing. Upon this, three Indians

[12] Emmerich's lieutenant reported two British, two Germans, thirty-seven Indians,
and a "number of Rebels" killed, with two natives and eight white Continentals
taken prisoner.

[13] Less than a year later, Major John Stewart of Maryland was among the first
Americans into the British works at Stony Point on the Hudson. Congress voted
him one of two gold medals struck to celebrate that inspiriting action.

[14] As did some Westchester volunteers under Captain David Williams.

[15] In 1765, Sachem Nimham, with two other Wappingers and their wives, was
received by George III at Windsor Castle and promised resolution of the natives'
land grievances by the Lords of Trade and Plantations. On the way home, he
attended Sunday church services at Gravesend. A deranged widow of a British soldier
who had been killed in North America attacked the Sachem, crying, "You murdered
my husband!" It created a near riot.

ventured to throw themselves upon the mercy of the British soldiers, and were immediately drawn out by the bridge, and there killed.

The following day, 1 September 1778, she had walked the battle site with her family:

I saw a great many dead Indians,[16] and one British trooper in particular who lay alongside a fence. He was a fine, tall splendid-looking young soldier, whose looks I have never forgotten. Several of the wounded were taken to the homes of Frederick and Daniel Devoe, where their wounds were dressed and cared for. One poor Indian was brought to the latter's house, a most distressing looking object, having one side of his face cleaved by a sabre cut almost to the chin. Here he was nursed several weeks until he was finally able to get away north to some of his comrades, with his face frightfully disfigured.[17]

The old chief Nimham was so badly wounded he must have soon after died, yet before his death he was still able to crawl down the hill to a running brook. There his body was found, by the peculiar action of the house dogs, which led to the suspicion they had eaten human flesh. They were followed, and the remains of Nimham's body, nearly devoured by dogs, was discovered, and also the mutilated bodies of two or three others.

They were all buried in the 'Indian Field,' with large stones piled on their graves, not so much as a monument but to protect their bodies from further desecration.

WITH THE DEATHS of Sachem Daniel Nimham, his two sons, and most of the adult males of the Wappinger Nation, the long legal battle to recover the lands stolen from them with invalid patents and forged deeds by the tory Philipse Family came to an end. At the start of the Revolution, the new State of New York had confiscated all Philipse property, and, on 22 October 1779, established a Commission of

---

[16] "Eighteen Indians were buried in one pit," wrote Robert Bolton seventy years later.

[17] This survivor may have been Job, described by Bolton as "living to a good old age, gaining his living by fishing on the banks of the Hudson. Whenever he could be tempted to relate the horrors of that day, big tears would start in his eyes and he would sob like a child.

Forfeiture to raise urgently needed public revenue by auctioning off parcels of land, mostly to former Philipse tenant farmers.

Mary Philipse had inherited Lots 3, 5, and 9, an even one-third (about 70,000 acres) of present day Putnam County, in 1754 from her Uncle Adolph, who died intestate and without issue. With her husband Colonel Roger Morris and their three children, she fled to England from New York City in 1782. There they petitioned for and received substantial compensation for their confiscated property. With the Wappingers gone from the scene, that might have ended the matter—except for an unusual legal tangle.

To satisfy ancient feudal provisions of entail for properly preserving and eventually bequeathing her land holdings, Roger Morris and Mary Philipse executed on 12 January 1758 a complicated prenuptial agreement in an elaborate land transfer ceremony.

Both Morrises were eventually "convicted and attainted of adhering to the enemy," and all their New York property was confiscated by the new State.[18]

The Morris children, however, were minors at the time of their parents' attainder. In that hectic Revolutonary period no one immediately realized that common law forbade "corruption of the blood," the transfer of parental guilt to a minor child. The legally innocent Morris children could not be deprived of their entailed right to inherit the real estate of their adjudged treasonous mother and father. Upon their parents' deaths, the children could legally repossess the land.

Provided, of course, that the new United States courts could be persuaded to so interpret Article V of the 3 September 1783 Treaty of Paris that ended the War of Independence and guaranteed the pre-Revolutionary property rights of otherwise peaceful citizens of Great Britain and the United States.

It was Aaron Burr, in 1809, who first realized this legislative oversight and called it to the attention of John Jacob Astor. Astor quickly sought out the three surviving Morris children in England— Joanna Morris Hincks (wife of Thomas Cowper Hincks), Maria Morris, and Commander Henry Gage Morris of the Royal Navy. Negotiating through British lawyers, Astor paid the children a total

---

[18] Besides the confiscation, in the earliest act of the Legislature, all adult male members of the Philipse Family were also threatened with death by hanging, without benefit of clergy, if caught within the revolutionary lines.

of $100,000 to "grant, bargain, sell, alienate, and release all reversionary rights" to one-third of Putnam County, New York.

Roger Morris died in 1794; all Astor had to do was sit back and wait for Mrs. Morris, whom Astor never met, to die as well. It was one of the slowest hatching nest eggs in legal history. Mary Philipse Morris lived to the ripe old age of ninety-five, expiring in London on 20 July 1825, a half century after the patriot militiamen first gathered on Lexington Green.

Meanwhile, Astor's "reversionary rights" continued to hang like Damocles's sword above the heads of several hundred farm families and other landholders in Putnam County—to say nothing of the head of every New York State taxpayer, who had to guarantee the land titles the Forfeiture Commissioners had sold in good faith forty years earlier.

In legal parlance, the taxpayers were threatened with having to "make Mr. Astor whole," if Astor could successfully litigate his claim to the lands with all improvements:

> Houses, cottages, outhouses, buildings, closes of land, meadow and pasture, woods and underwoods, the grounds and soil thereof, hedges, ditches, fences, mounds, ways, passages, waters, lands covered with water, watercourses, liberties, millages, easements, profits, commodities, advantages, emoluments and appurtenances, whatsoever.

More than a decade had passed since the conclusion of a second war with Great Britain, and life in the United States had returned to normal. A deal was whispered long in advance of Mrs. Morris's death. Upon her demise, Astor would bring a test "suit in ejectment" against a representative group of Putnam County farmers, carrying it to the United States Supreme Court on appeal if necessary. If Astor finally lost the case, he would have to go away, having lost both his original stake and legal costs as well.

Should Astor win, the State of New York would have to pay him $450,000, a rather impressive return on his investment, in exchange for which Astor would execute valid titles for everyone living on the former Morris lands.

The jury found for Astor in *Astor vs. James Carver, Samuel Kelly, Nathaniel Crane, et al.*, in the New York Federal Court in 1827. In

1828, with Daniel Webster appearing for New York State, the United States Supreme Court, under Chief Justice John Marshall, affirmed the almost half-million dollar verdict.

Before long, like Frederick Philipse III before him, Astor was the richest man in America.

In Putnam County, local politicians named one of his nation's mountains for Daniel Nimham.

# CHAPTER XI

# General Sullivan's Old Squaw

*IN WHICH a "little campaign" between the Continental Army and British-led Native American opponents balances some long-remembered cruelties.*

*TWO POLICIES* in particular of the British War Office fueled the American will to fight at a flash point throughout the eight years of the Revolution: one was the British employment, with deadly effect, of great numbers of German-speaking mercenary troops (hired by the King without Parliamentary approval, and eventually adding up to a third of the royal forces in America), and the other was the encouragement, through subsidies, of hundreds and often thousands of Native Americans to attack the influx of patriot settlers along the western state frontiers. As a result, brutal hand-to-hand combat raged unremittingly between the original inhabitants of these lands and their dispossessors. News and rumors of each successive horror quickly spread throughout the seaboard. Among the most notorious of these border raids by combined tory and Native American forces were those in 1778 launched against the Wyoming Valley settlements near the northern Pennsylvania border and the attacks that devastated Cherry Valley in New York State. In both actions, hundreds of Iroquois warriors demonstrated their loyalty to the British crown.

*ON 25 FEBRUARY 1779*, General Washington responded to mounting pressure from the inhabitants of the same Wyoming Valley area where Margaret Corbin lost both her parents (see *Chapter VII*) to

Native American raiding parties. The great West Point Chain, installed a year previous (see *Chapter XII*), was now successfully blocking the British naval strategy of splitting the Americans along the line of the Hudson River. Congress had long called for a punitive strike at the tribal lands of Great Britain's Iroquois allies (see *Chapter II*, note 5), in the fertile Finger Lakes region of west-central New York State. Now the relatively quiescent military situation in the northern states permitted a sizable expedition into what seaboard city dwellers liked to call the "back country," to "chastise the savages who have been ravaging homes for many months."

Washington assured Philadelphia that he was planning such a campaign, detaching almost 4,000 Continental soldiers and artillerymen. For political reasons, the commander in chief first offered leadership of this mission to his annoying military rival, fifty-one-year-old General Horatio Gates, then commanding in Boston. Gates huffily and tardily declined the assignment, saying he no longer had the "youth and strength" for such arduous service. Washington thereupon turned to a man twelve years Gates's junior, New Hampshire General John Sullivan, a lawyer in civilian life and the son of indentured Irish servants who had come to New England in 1723.

The commander cautioned Sullivan to keep his preparations and final destination secret, since a principal aim of the expedition would be to take "as many prisoners of every age and sex as possible" to serve as hostages to assure the future good behavior of the Iroquois. But with tory sympathizers scattered throughout Sullivan's staging areas, the purpose and swelling size of the expedition could not remain hidden.

In April 1779, operations commenced against four nations of the Iroquois Confederacy—the Oneidas and Tuscaroras defied Mohawk pressure and supported the Revolution—and a preliminary raid from Fort Schuyler by 558 Americans under Colonel Goose van Schaick destroyed the Onondaga villages south of present-day Syracuse. By 17 June, General James Clinton had left Canajoharie on the Mohawk River and, with 1,400 men, was making his way twenty miles southwest to Otsego Lake.[1]

---

[1] Within a decade, William Cooper, father of James Fennimore, would move his family here from New Jersey, creating the village of Cooperstown.

Lieutenant Thomas Machin, his West Point Chain now fixed stoutly across the Hudson River (see *Chapter XII*), accompanied General Clinton as an engineering aide. At the outlet to the lake, Clinton waited six weeks for a signal from Sullivan to float 125 miles down the Susquehanna River and join forces with Sullivan's 2,312 troops at Teaogo [Tioga, now Athens, Pennsylvania] on the upper Delaware across the Pennsylvania border.

The orders from Sullivan finally arrived on 9 August in what had been a very lean year for American military successes. (The only bright spot had been General Anthony Wayne's 16 July midnight capture of Stony Point on the Hudson River.) By 22 August, Clinton's men had made contact with Sullivan's troops, who had moved slowly north more than 150 miles from Easton, Pennsylvania, on the lower Delaware, building their own military road as they advanced.

The American troops were no longer the volunteer farm boys who four years earlier had dropped their plow reins and streamed onto Charlestown Neck, nor were they the raw recruits who had scrabbled together fortifications on Brooklyn and Washington Heights to face down the greatest army the world had ever seen. They were now veterans, in a combat-ready, relatively well-trained and disciplined fighting force. The soldiers felt themselves to be—and were—superior to any combination their enemies might field against them.

Leaving Tioga on 26 August, Sullivan's unified army reorganized as four brigades under Generals William Maxwell, Enoch Poor, Edward Hand, and Clinton, respectively. The combined American force marched north through the Chemung River Valley. The Iroquois families, warned of the Continentals' progress by each day's traditional morning gun, withdrew into the surrounding forest, making hostage-taking impossible. The natives quickly realized that Sullivan's 3,700 men[2] were more than just a raiding party, to which they were long accustomed, but were a force strong enough to wipe out their society. The Americans were not merely passing through.

On 29 August, at the Native American village of Newtown on the Chemung River, just below present-day Elmira, 500 Iroquois warriors laid an ambush for Sullivan's army. The natives' leaders

---

[2] Equal to more than one-third of the total Iroquois population of New York State.

included the influential Thayendanegea (the Mohawk sachem Joseph Brant—see *Chapter II, Note 13*). The natives also were supported by two battalions of British Rangers, fifteen Regulars from the British 8th Regiment, and 200 of Sir Guy Johnson's Royal Green tories, all commanded by Captain Walter Butler. At Newtown, the King's troops and their native allies erected hidden barricades. In the bitter forest fight that followed, in which three Continentals were killed and thirty-nine wounded, the American cannon helped to rout the outnumbered enemy. The decisive contest put an end to further argument among the natives on whether to stand and fight or simply to melt away in front of the hard-driving Americans.

William Barton served as a lieutenant in the 1st New Jersey Regiment of Maxwell's 1st Brigade. He wrote in his diary:

> Sent out a small party to look for some of the dead Indians. Toward noon they found them and skinned two of them from their hips down for boot leggings; one pair for the Major [Daniel Platt], the other for myself.

Organized Iroquois resistance to Sullivan's advance dissolved after the Battle of Newtown. Native crops and villages were abandoned to the American ax and torch. Sullivan's troops (who relied on their own set of Oneida guides and interpreters) destroyed the extensive and fruitful vegetable fields previously tended by Iroquois women. The gardens had been filled with beans, peas, squash, potatoes, pumpkins, watermelons, cucumbers, and other produce in wide variety, as well as enormous quantities of corn—Sullivan estimated 160,000 bushels. To the soldiers' amazement, some of those carefully cultivated ears of corn were almost two feet long. Apple, peach, and pear orchards were chopped down. As the late historian Page Smith observed, "The business of this campaign proved a strange task indeed for American men at arms—a warfare against fruits and vegetables."

*ON 2 SEPTEMBER 1779*, three days after the Battle of Newtown, Sullivan's vanguard of light infantry under General Hand entered the empty village of Shequaga, or Catherine's Town, a few miles below present-day Watkins Glen. The place had been named after Catherine Montour, a French-Canadian woman who had married the Seneca sachem Telenemut and settled with him at Shequaga, where they farmed and became successful horse breeders. A captain in the 3rd New Hampshire Regiment made a note in his journal that Catherine had been "debauched by an Indian chief; afterwards marrying him, and made queen of the place."

All but one native at Shequaga, including a "Dutch family who lived here, with a number of feather beds in their house," had fled before the American advance. The native who remained was an Iroquois woman too aged and feeble to flee. More than any other native Sullivan and his soldiers encountered, this ancient representative of an indigenous culture effected the American soldiers. Almost thirty of them wrote about her.

Twenty-eight-year-old Lieutenant Colonel Henry Dearborn commanded the 3rd New Hampshire Regiment in Poor's 2nd Brigade. Trained as a physician, he had participated in many previous battles and campaigns, beginning with Bunker Hill and including Arnold's wilderness march on Quebec, during which he was captured. Exchanged in 1777, Dearborn fearlessly distinguished himself at Saratoga, and survived Valley Forge and Monmouth. He became the best known of the Sullivan expedition's many diarists.[3]

He wrote in his diary:

> A very old Squaw was found in the bushes who was not able to go off with the rest. She says the Squaws & young indians were very loath to quit the town but were for giving themselves up, but the warriors would not agree to it.

John Burrowes served as a Captain of the 5th New Jersey Regiment in Maxwell's 1st Brigade. He wrote:

> One of the soldiers found at this place this morning an old squaw in a bunch of bushes, she not being able to go off with them, was hid there to be safe. She is the greatest picture of old age I ever saw. The General sent for her, she was carried to his marque [tent]. The poor old creature was just ready to die with fear, thinking she was to be killed. She informed the General that there was a great debate

---

[3] Later, after serving two terms in Congress, Dearborn was appointed Jefferson's Secretary of War, in which capacity he formulated a plan to resettle all Native Americans west of the Mississippi River.

between the warriors, their squaws and children. The squaws had a mind to stay at home with their children. It was carried to such a length that the warriors were obliged to threaten to scalp the women if they did not go.

Twenty-year-old Erkules Beatty served as a 2nd Lieutenant and Paymaster of the 4th Pennsylvania Regiment in Hand's 3rd Brigade. Back in April, he had participated in the destruction of the Onondaga villages south of Oneida Lake. He wrote:

This morning a very aged Squaw was found in a Corn field who was not able to get off, for Age. She was brought in and She told us that the warriors had stayed in the town till Near night before they went away. There was another Squaw found in the woods who pretended she was lame & the Soldier came home to get some others to help fetch her in & when they returned the Squaw had hid away & they could not find her. The old Squaw after She was examined at Hd. Quarters, they was going to send her to the Indians but she was so old she could not ride. From her looks and what we could learn she must be I think above 120 years old. Our Indians built a house for her & we Gave her provision & left her.

Thirty-year-old Captain Jeremiah Fogg, a Harvard graduate and Paymaster of the 2nd New Hampshire Regiment, served also as an aide-de-camp to General Poor. Fogg wrote:

Early this morning we found in a bark hut an awful object, and upon examination it appeared to be Madame Sacho, one of the Tuscarora nation, whose silver locks, wrinkled face, dim eyes and curvitude of body denoted her to be a full blooded antidiluvian hag! Her language was very little understood by our interpreters. However, one of our Oneidas could understand her and communicated to her in his own language. She gave the following account, viz: That she was left by necessity, and expected to have been killed, and seemed thankful that the good spirit had influenced our great chief to save her; that the squaws and the little ones were anxious for peace, but that Butler had told them they would all be put to death.

LEAVING CATHERINE'S TOWN, Sullivan's army moved north along Seneca Creek and Seneca Lake to the native villages of Kanadaseagea and Schoyere. There they destroyed more than fifty dwellings before turning west towards other Finger Lakes settlements. The substantial cabins and homes in these established communities were framed in the colonial manner of axe-hewn timbers, faced with peeled bark slabs or milled and painted boards. A few were stoutly built with stone walls, many with fireplaces, brick or stone chimneys, and glazed windows. Complete with colonial furniture, the Iroquois housing adopted much of the colonists' standards of living. They ate with pewter spoons and forks from glazed earthenware. Sullivan called some of the dwellings "very elegant."

Many of the natives had adopted colonial dress. They raised milch and beef cattle, and used horses or oxen to plow their fertile grain-fields.

On 15 September, Washington amplified his original order to Sullivan with "points which I may not have sufficiently expressed in my general instructions, or if I have, which I wish to repeat." They were aimed at making the "destruction of the native settlements so final and complete as to put it out of their power to derive the smallest succor from them." Accordingly, Sullivan's army continued west, destroying Canandaigua, Honeoye, and Kanagha.

Cruelty escalates cruelty. Under the unrelenting pressure of Sullivan's organized devastation, the most "civilized" Native American nation on the continent finally demonstrated an unspeakable barbarism. On 13 September, they annihilated a rashly extended Continental scouting party[4] near the Seneca villages on the Genesee River—the expedition's "farthest west." Sullivan destroyed Genesee

---

[4] The partially skinned body of the group's leader, Lieutenant Thomas Boyd, was found with his genitals placed in the mouth of his severed head. The popular Boyd had been captured at Quebec on New Year's Eve 1775 and had remained a British prisoner of war for two years, until exchanged. The discovery of his mutilated remains staggered Sullivan's army. But the atrocity was hardly without precedent in colonial North America, according to the sensational pamphlet "Breeden Raedt" (General Advice), an anonymous attack on the Dutch West India Company printed in Antwerp in 1649. Five years before then, and before the British siezed New Netherland from the Dutch, Governor Willem Kieft's townsfolk apparently watched with satisfaction as Dutch soldiers emasculated a live Canarsie captive, placed his genitals in his mouth, and then decapitated him. Adrienne Culville Damen was carried away by the spectacle. She began to kick the severed head like a football up and down New Amsterdam's Broad Street.

Castle, a Seneca village of 128 wooden and stone houses that he described as "beautifully situated."

*THE EXPEDITION* then turned back towards Tioga, with two detachments circling eastward to burn the Cayuga and Lower Mohawk villages. By 23 September, Sullivan's main force again passed through Catherine's Town, where three weeks before they had left the old native woman sitting in her hut.

Captain Burrowes wrote in his diary:

We find the old squaw that we had left when going, gave her a quantity of flour and meat, a blanket and knife. The young squaw that had come to take care of the old one after we had passed through, we found shot and thrown into a mudhole, supposed to be done by some of the soldiers.

Lieutenant Beatty wrote:

We buried the lame Squaw which I mentioned on our going, it is supposed she was Shot by some of our men. The Old Squaw that we left here had built or got built a neat little bark hutt where she lived. The General ordered to be left her almost a keg of flower and some meat which was done, and I suppose she will live in splendour.

Lieutenant William Barton, who had earlier accepted the present of native-skin boot legs from his scouting party, wrote:

Found the old squaw here which was left when we went up, with a paper that had many lines of Indian wrote underneath as protection that was given her by the General, the contents of which I did not hear. We also found the corpse of a young squaw who appeared to have been shot three or four days, which lay in a mud hole; supposed to have come there since our departure, to take care of the old brute. Who killed her I cannot ascertain, but it is generally believed to have been three men of ours who were sent up from Tioga on express a few days before. At our departure from here the General ordered there should be left a keg of pork and some biscuit, &c. for the old creature to subsist on, although it was so scarce an article that no one under the rank of field officer had ever tasted any since leaving Tioga.

Captain Fogg recounted:

We found the old squaw just as we left her twenty days before in her bark hut, with a quart of corn by her. It appears that there had been a young squaw with her, whom we found dead forty yards distant; supposed to have been shot by some of our expresses a few days before. The old one, from her appearance, must have been ninety years old. Such is the enmity of our soldiery against the savages, that they would readily have murdered this helpless impotent wretch. But the common dictates of humanity, a veneration for old age and a regard for the female world of any age and denomination induced our General to spare her, giving her the choice of going with the army, or remaining in her wigwam, with a month's provisions; and she preferred the latter.

Two days earlier, Colonel Henry Dearborn and his 3rd New Hampshire Regiment "were order'd to proceed to the west side of Kaiyugea [Cayuga] Lake to burn and destroy what Settlements might still be found." On 22 September, Dearborn, whom a recent Jefferson biographer has called "cool, collected, and kindly," came across "a wigwam with 3 Squaws and one young Indian who was a cripple. I took two of the Squaws," writes the Colonel. "They were about 40 or 50 years old, and we march'd on about 3 miles and found one hut, which I burnt." According to Dearborn's diary entry, the hut was empty.

But Lieutenant Barton's journal tells a different story:

Sunday 26th [September]—The detachment under Col. Durbin [Dearborn] that came down the Kihuga lake, arrived with two squaws, and inform'd us they burnt three or four towns. They likewise say they found one other Indian with the old squaw, the latter so old as not to be able to be brought off; the Indian man was young but decrepid to such a degree that he could not walk. I have since heard it said, the Colonel left one house standing for them to stay in, and would not suffer them to be hurt, but some of the soldiers, taking an opportunity when not observed, set the house on fire, after securing and making the door fast.

Somewhere along the American chain of command, Sullivan's order had been ignored. The venerable woman was burned alive.

*IN LESS THAN* one month, losing, Sullivan boasted, only forty men on a march of 280 miles, the Revolutionary forces managed to burn the homes and crops of forty major Iroquois towns in western New York State. The dispossessed natives were forced to take winter refuge with the British at Fort Niagara, where they were inadequately fed, clothed, and sheltered in an encampmemt racked by disease.

By the end of the war, the approximately 10,000 Iroquois men, women, and children in New York State had been reduced to 5,000. On 20 October 1779, summarizing results, Washington wrote to Lafayette, complaining that Sullivan's expedition had "failed in the main purpose" by not having "done more in taking hostages," even though he had "disconcerted and humbled" the native population. The comment leaked, and an irritated Sullivan resigned from the army a month later.

The British-led native fighting forces on the frontier were not destroyed and, to Washington's ill-concealed disappointment, almost no Iroquois hostages were captured. But the natives were driven from their ancestral habitations just before the harvest and the hard winter of 1779-1780.

The Iroquois nations remained united, however, firmly defending the King's cause. From Fort Niagara, exasperated and vengeful, they would sally forth in 1780 and 1781, still led by Joseph Brant, to again ravage the frontier settlements, with greater malignity than ever.

*JOINING THE CELEBRATION* of the Elmira, New York, 1879 American Revolutionary Centennial—a century after Sullivan's Expedition and three years after Custer's debacle on the Little Big Horn—a group of dignitaries spoke before a large crowd on the Newtown battlefield. General Henry Warner Slocum had agreed to address the gathering, followed by William Tecumseh Sherman .

Slocum had been born nearby, on New York land taken from the Onondaga nation. His reputation as a patriot was impeccable. He had enjoyed a distinguished military career in the Seminole War, and had subsequently commanded Sherman's left wing on the 1864 March to the Sea. Slocum concluded his comments by comparing Sullivan's 1779 campaign to Sherman's still controversial devastation in Georgia.

"But I say to you," Slocum thundered, "that Sherman's army never committed the atrocities that were committed by General Sullivan's."

The comparison apparently rubbed Sherman the wrong way. The fifty-nine-year-old former commander of the Army of the Tennessee minced no words. Turning his back on his former subordinate, Sherman said:

> I know it is a very common, too common, practice to accuse General Sullivan of having destroyed peach trees and cornfields, and all that nonsense. Sullivan had to do it—and he did it. Whenever all things ought to be peaceful, war comes and purifies the atmosphere. . . .
>
> Ever since the first white man landed upon this continent, there has been a battle. We are in that same war today—a war between civilization, and savages. The same men, endowed by the same feelings that General Sullivan's army had, are today contending with the same causes, and the same races—two thousand miles west of here—to prepare the way for that civilization that must go along, wherever yonder flag floats.

Sherman concluded:

> If our young men in the East would go out there, and lay the foundation for future States and future homes, that would be all the battle—and we would not have so much growling about Indians and Negroes, and other questions that disturb our politicians today.

His words were met with warm applause.

*A YEAR LATER*, in a more reflective moment, Sherman observed: "War is hell." It was reminiscent of an observation by Robert E. Lee in the middle of the Civil War: "It is well that war is so terrible—we should grow too fond of it."

# CHAPTER XII

# The Great
# Chain Robbery

*IN WHICH a gullible group of American curio collectors illustrates
Jeremiah (5.21): "O foolish people. . .which have eyes, and see not!"*

*MIDWAY THROUGH* the War of Independence, on 30 April 1778, the
American Revolutionaries succeeded in stringing a massive floating
chain across the Hudson River at West Point. Quickly dubbed
"General Washington's Watch Chain" by the Continental soldiers,
the unusual obstruction denied use of this strategic waterway to the
British for the remainder of the war. The chain's 800 wrought iron
links, supported by and connecting forty huge log rafts, were hastily
forged at nearby Sterling Furnace in the Ramapo Mountains. Each
two-foot-long link weighed about 125 pounds.

Installation of the chain was supervised by thirty-three-year-old
artillery engineer Thomas Machin[1] of Boston. He had "gone out with
the Tea Party" in 1773 and, two years later, laid out overnight the
American fortification on Breed's (Bunker) Hill. Lieutenant Machin
was a well-educated English immigrant with practical experience in
civil engineering. In the spring of 1777, he had succeeded in stretching
a light chained boom across the Hudson River near Bear Mountain.
Within six months, that obstruction was outflanked and destroyed
by British land forces under Sir Henry Clinton.

---

[1] In the summer of 1779, Machin was promoted to captain and served under General
James Clinton on the Sullivan Expedition against the Iroquois.

Racing against a manufacturing deadline, Machin had the new
and far heavier replacement at West Point strung like pearls on a
necklace 1,500 feet across the river between cannon batteries on the
west shore and Constitution Island. Early each winter for the next
four years, the West Point garrison hauled the 300 tons of wrought
iron chain and log rafts out of the clutches of tidal river ice and
restrung them the following spring. It was always a freezing, back-
breaking job.

The chain survived an unsuccessful sabotage attempt by Benedict
Arnold in 1780, but, most significantly, it was never directly chal-
lenged by a single Royal Navy warship. So perfectly did it perform
its function of blocking the Hudson River and Valley, and, by
extension, the entire Northeast, from further British incursion that
it effectively drove the next five years of conflict to the Southern
states, unquestionably shortening the war. Indeed, it was no accident
that the final major Northern battle—an enemy delaying action in
New Jersey—came only three months after the West Point Chain
was successfully installed.

When the war ended, the chain represented too much valuable
scrap iron to be allowed simply to rust in peace. A handful of its links
were saved and set aside, thirteen of which, one for each original state,
are still on display at the Military Academy. Refreshed each year by
a coat of shiny black enamel, the section of preserved linkage continues to intrigue untold numbers of Military Academy visitors. The
remainder of the chain was relegated to the West Point Foundry
furnaces at nearby Cold Spring, New York, to be melted down for
other uses.

CONSIDERING THAT the iron left from Captain Machin's Hudson
River barrier represents the United States's most famous Revolutionary War memento, it is not surprising that a pair of enterprising
bunco artists attempted—and succeeded at—stealing it for their own.

John C. Abbey was a thirty-five-year-old New York "odds-and-
ends man" with a keen sense of history. This New York City junk
dealer customarily went under the more colorful Christian appellation of Westminster. "For fifty years," said The New York Times, "it
was a byword along the East River waterfront that you could get
anything from a nail to a cannon at Westminster Abbey's old
place"—including fully authenticated links of the West Point Chain.

His was certainly one of the heaviest con games ever practiced, in its own way the equivalent of selling the Brooklyn Bridge.

How Abbey claimed he obtained his links made a colorful story. In the 1880s, he said, they had surfaced from the innermost recesses of the 300-acre Brooklyn Navy Yard. In fact, they were eighty-six links of a heavy contemporary rolled-steel mooring ground anchor chain. This type of chain, manufactured exclusively in Great Britain, was used to stabilize large steamship mooring buoys in ports around the world without pier facilities.

Although the genuine links of the West Point Chain were easily available for comparison at the United States Military Academy only fifty miles up the Hudson, the junk dealer began to peddle his scrap metal as the real thing to unsophisticated buyers across the country.

It was a startling parody of what Van Wyck Brooks once characterized as America's "search for a useable past," or, as a more recent writer suggests in a hagiographic study of George Washington, it answers "a specific human need to achieve a measure of material intimacy with great events."

IN 1900, a former New York City mayor, Abram Hewitt, purchased some of the links from Abbey. Twenty-six of these still grace the front lawn of Hewett's former estate at Ringwood Manor, now a northwestern New Jersey state park. Ringwood's smooth, neatly chamfered links are not only three times heavier than the rugged links hurriedly forged in 1778 at Sterling Furnace; they are also on average sixty-five percent longer and an additional three and three-quarter inches in circumference.

Hewitt, himself an experienced ironmaster, lived only a few hours' carriage ride from West Point. Eventually the ex-mayor got around to comparing his links with those on Trophy Point at the Military Academy, and was soon loudly (and unsuccessfully) demanding his money back. Hewitt complained that Abbey had "sold the chain to me on false representation."

Some of Hewitt's links eventually found their way to Orange County's Museum Village, a historic restoration at Monroe, New York, where they are still displayed (unlabeled) on the village green.

Almost a half century later, Hewitt's son Edward wrote in a private memoir how a visiting "English iron manufacturer recognized [the Abbey chain] as one of the Admiralty buoy chains made by his firm, which had been used in New York harbor." (An Admiralty chain had to pass prescribed strength tests at a British naval testing facility.) The younger Hewitt also related how he had quietly "analyzed the iron of the links and found it to be Lowmoor iron from England."

For several decades, Edward Hewitt kept those embarassing identifications to himself. Contemporary metallurgical evidence now supports his assertion that Westminster Abbey's so-called "West Point Chain" was never wrought in a Ramapo Mountain Furnace in 1778, but was manufactured more than a century later at Brown, Lenox & Co.'s Newbridge Chain and Anchor Works at Pontypridd, fifteen miles north of Cardiff, Wales, along the Glamorganshire Canal.

*IN THE EARLY 1900s*, Abbey's counterfeit chain enterprise was taken over by neighboring businessman Francis Bannerman. Born in Scotland in 1851 and brought to America as a youngster, Bannerman had become one of the country's major surplus arms dealers. As the new and better organized proprietor of the false West Point Chain, Bannerman celebrated his takeover by publishing a little pamphlet, "History of the Great Iron Chain Laid Across the Hudson River in 1778, by Order of General George Washington." Bannerman spun his own fascinating story, still naively recited by a few historians, about how the bulk of the West Point Chain links finally ended their days at the Brooklyn Navy Yard.

Much of the chain, according to Bannerman, had actually escaped the scrap furnace to lay stored at West Point for almost a century. Then, in March 1864, near the end of the Civil War, a hundred or so chain links were barged down the Hudson for display at the famous New York Metropolitan Fair. The event was a great success, raising over one million dollars to care for the Union wounded. At the Fair's conclusion (Bannerman recounted), the Great Chain links were not returned to the United States Military Academy, but were ferried across the East River to the Brooklyn Yard.

Bannerman's pamphlet then leaps ahead two decades, to the time when his "Revolutionary relics" could be safely exhumed. During Grover Cleveland's first administration, says Bannerman, the Navy Department took steps to consolidate all its various quartermaster installations into one vast General Storekeepers Department. "In time," Bannerman continues, the Navy "found this old chain and without either knowing the history or having any appreciation for such a valuable relic, ordered it sold at auction, September 4, 1887." Bannerman tells how, twenty-two years after the end of the Civil War, the unusual links were bid for by his own father, Francis, Sr., from whom they were subsequently purchased by Westminster Abbey. Abbey, relates Bannerman, then sold sections of his West Point Chain to the public "for about 10 years."

HAVING BOUGHT Abbey's chain, Bannerman continued to peddle it on a much wider scale. Two links, his pamphlet notes, were sold to Colonel Robert Townsend of Oyster Bay, New York, a credulous great-grandson of the original Sterling Furnace ironmaster. Three others went to Townsend descendants in Danbury, Connecticut, and Allegheny, Pennsylvania.

Another of Bannerman's links, sold to Daniel Jackson Townsend, a descendant in Niagara Falls, was subsequently presented by his heirs to the Buffalo and Erie County Historical Society, which currently lists it as "one of the most historic articles in our museum."

During the 1933 commencement exercises at the United States Coast Guard Academy in New London, Connecticut, six links Bannerman sold many years before to still another Townsend descendant were presented to the Academy by the ironmaster's great-granddaughter. Originally mounted on the stone wall of the Academy's athletic field, the links now rest on the floor inside the front entrance to the Academy's museum.

Thirteen of Bannerman's remaining links were sold to millionaire Edward F. Searles, a Massachusetts interior decorator who married Mark Hopkins's widow, thereby gaining control of her Central Pacific Railroad fortune. Searles came to Bannerman seeking additional decoration for an elaborate statue of George Washington that already graced a corner of his Methuen, Massachusetts, estate. The rear of the overladen marble and bronze monument was soon bedecked with thirteen Bannerman links—again, one for each original state.

Sixty years later, in 1958, a Searles descendant sold that huge statue plus seven of its "West Point" links to Forest Lawn Memorial Park in Los Angeles, California. The links, now separated from the statue, are installed in a mislabeled niche in the cemetery's Glendale

"Court of Freedom, beyond the Mystery of Life Garden, where Cathedral Drive becomes the High Road."

At the time of Searles's purchase, Bannerman also sold four links to Westchester executive John H. Starin, who then donated them to the Glen Island Museum in Pelham, New York. When the museum was demolished in 1921 by the Westchester County Park Commission to make way for a casino and recreational park, the links were auctioned for $500.

Their new owner was a British businessman, Sir Henry S. Wellcome, who outbid the New-York Historical Society. Within a year, Wellcome donated his prize to the Smithsonian Institution. By then, the New-York Historical Society's secretary had begun to suspect the provenance of the Bannerman links, and relayed his doubts to the secretary of the Smithsonian—who did not respond. (Today those Smithsonian links are quietly stashed away in a Maryland warehouse.)

*TWENTY ADDITIONAL* links passed, through the hands of an insatiable midwestern antiques collector, to the Chicago Historical Society, where they are now unceremoniously dumped, like a gigantic monkey-puzzle, in the shrubbery outside the Society's back door.

To close out his inventory of "Great West Point Chain links," Bannerman hit on an ingenious and lucrative scheme to dispose of all the "damaged" opened links left behind whenever chain sections were sold. Bannerman carved up all his leftovers into "handsome souvenir desk weights."

Each link yielded several hundred blanks; the pieces were machined, polished, and engraved "SECTION OF CHAIN / USED BY GENL. GEO. WASHINGTON / WEST POINT, N.Y. 1778." A round "handle," actually a surplus one and one-quarter-inch Civil War canister shot, was welded to the desk weight. Bannerman charged $2.75 for the finished weight, and threw in his eight-page pamphlet. Chopped into such tiny bits, each chain link brought Bannerman a total of almost $350, a considerable improvement over Abbey's original wholesale price—"five (5) cents net cash per pound."

*WITHOUT EXCEPTION,* writers on the West Point chain swallowed any misgivings regarding the illogical size, shape, and appearance of the Abbey/Bannerman links. A few researchers were willing to acknowledge some problems with certain details, but no one cared to sail into the wind of "received historic fact." One of the country's most respected civil engineers wrote shortly after World War II: "The appearance of some of the large links is certainly a bit suspicious," but he still refused to acknowledge their obvious manufacture in a 19th century rolling mill.

He even went so far as to assert that in the midst of a desperate revolution, the neat "chamfers on the 3-1/2" bar [almost forty feet of chamfering to each of several hundred links] were done with a hand hammer."

Around the same time, a Columbia University engineering instructor requested permission from the Hewitt family to conduct a metallurgical experiment on one of those Ringwood Manor links. Approval was refused, but the instructor machined and polished a Bannerman paperweight instead, and published eight photomicrographs in an iron trades magazine.

Ken Holloway, retired Chain and Smiths Manager of the Welsh Pontypridd works, assisted me in interpreting those photomicrographs, describing the traditional 19th-century Brown, Lenox processes for manufacturing ground mooring chain links:

> Iron scrap of known quality was piled into box piles, risen to welding temperature, and forged into slabs under the steam hammer. Those slabs were again raised to welding temperature and forged into a larger slab, which was passed through rolls to reduce it to bar size and shape. I was able to watch this process of making square chain right up to the second World War.

The Columbia instructor independently determined that the "iron was forged first in several pieces, then bundled together and welded into one large piece." Such an analysis in no way describes the original Sterling West Point Chain raw materials, or any forging process known in 1778. The instructor still failed to draw the obvious conclusion.

BANNERMAN DIED in November 1918, at the end of World War I, exhausted, said *The New York Times*, from his dedicated efforts to supply the British government with second-hand armaments "worth

almost three million dollars." *The Times* added, somewhat unchari-
tably for an obituary: "It was charged in Congress last summer that
Mr. Bannerman was trying to sell the United States Government for
$450,000, thirty six-inch guns bought by him from the Navy for
about $78 apiece."

Westminster Abbey outlived his more enterprising associate by
four years. "WESTMINSTER ABBEY DEAD," read the headline
over his obituary in *The New York Times* on 11 June 1922. The
subheadline read:"Old Front Street Ship Chandler Whose Warehouse was Famous."

But it took three more decades for truth to overtake the Ab-
bey/Bannerman chain myth. Not until the late 1980s did my enjoyable research in Wales finally make it clear that, if you want to look
upon Captain Machin's wonderful West Point Chain, you must skip
all those curious sections of Welsh mooring links at Forest Lawn,
Ringwood Manor, Museum Village, Oyster Bay, the Coast Guard
Academy, the Smithsonian warehouse, and the Chicago, Buffalo-and-
Erie-County, and Methuen Historical Societies.

Go to West Point instead, and marvel at the real thing—while
whistling "Yankee Doodle."

# Epilogue

*THE REVOLUTION came to an end, as eventually did all of its participants. But many lived to an advanced age, watching the country grow up.*

DAVID SALISBURY FRANKS served as a diplomatic courier during the close of the war and then briefly as American vice consul in Marseilles. He died of yellow fever in Philadelphia in 1793, at fifty-one. To avoid a pauper's field burial, friends arranged for his interment in the Christ Episcopal Churchyard.

JOHN SULLIVAN, after quitting the army, became active in Federalist politics and served as governor of New Hampshire from 1786 to 1789. He helped suppress Daniel Shays's agrarian rebellion in 1787. He died in 1795, at the age of fifty-five.

GEORGE WASHINGTON served eight years as president under the new Constitution and then retired to his Potomac estate. He was the nation's first—and only—universally beloved political leader. He died in 1799, at the age of sixty-seven.

MARGARET COCHRAN CORBIN died near West Point, apparently of alcoholism, in 1800, at the age of forty-nine. Her remains were reburied at the Military Academy Cemetery in 1926.

BENEDICT ARNOLD, after leading British military raids against his former comrades along the Northern and Southern coastlines, was welcomed in England and received approximately $100,000 for his treason. He became a successful merchant shipper in New Brunswick and fathered four sons who later joined the British army. He died in England in 1801, at sixty. Three years later, Peggy Shippen Arnold, at forty-four, died in London of uterine cancer.

ALEXANDER HAMILTON, after five years on Washington's wartime staff, finally saw action at the siege of Yorktown. After the Revolution, his political acumen made him a Founding Father, with an indomitable faith in the future United States as a great manufacturing nation. Hamilton served six years as Washington's Secretary of the Treasury. He was fatally wounded in a duel with Aaron Burr in 1804, at the age of forty-seven.

JOHN GRAVES SIMCOE served five years (from 1791) as Lieutenant Governor of Upper Canada and Ontario, during which time he almost brought on a precursor to the War of 1812. He continually incited native attack against American frontier settlements. Returning to England in 1796, he wrote his memoirs and became active in the Napoleonic wars. He died in 1806, at the age of fifty-four.

JOSEPH BRANT (*Thayendanegea*) continued in his role as the most influential Iroquois leader and spokesman. For twenty years after the Revolution, he urged other eastern Native American nations to peacefully negotiate with various United States treaty commissioners. He was invited to confer with President Washington in Philadelphia in 1792. Brant died at his home in Ontario in 1807, at the age of sixty-five.

COUNT RUMFORD (nee BENJAMIN THOMPSON) died near Paris in 1814, at the age of fifty-nine. He left a substantial bequest to Harvard College, but never returned to the land of his birth.

THOMAS MACHIN was awarded by General Washington the honor of firing the first cannon at the Siege of Yorktown. Machin went bankrupt in his post-war business of printing states' currency and minting coinage. He died in upstate New York in 1816, at the age of seventy-two.

OBADIAH BROWN farmed and raised a family near Albany, New York. He died in 1818, at the age of sixty-four.

DEBORAH SAMPSON GANNETT raised three children, and, for a brief period, toured the Northeast, recounting her unique wartime service. She died, ill and poor, in 1827, at the age of sixty-seven. In World War II, a Liberty Ship proudly bore her name.

HENRY DEARBORN pursued a long and relatively distinguished military/political career. A log fort named for him was the first structure of Chicago. He became Jefferson's Secretary of War, and, after his poor leadership in the War of 1812, served two years as Monroe's Minister to Portugal. He died in 1829, at the age of seventy-eight.

RICHARD VARICK became Washington's confidential secretary during and after the war. Later he entered politics and was elected mayor of New York City in 1789. He was founder and first president of the American Bible Society. He died in 1831, at seventy-eight.

MARY LUDWIG HAYS (*"Molly Pitcher"*) died in 1832, at the age of eighty-eight. She is memorialized by two bronze plaques (one recently stolen) at wellsprings on the Monmouth battlefield.

BANASTRE TARLETON, captured with Cornwallis at Yorktown, was paroled and returned to England before the end of the war. He served in Parliament from 1790 to 1812 and wrote his memoirs. He died in 1833, at the age of seventy-nine.

JOHN JACOB ASTOR was fifteen when the Wappingers were massacred at Indian Field. The remnants of Nimham's Nation, whose land Astor used as a massive 1828 real estate grubstake, were slowly absorbed into the Oneida Nation, drifting westward with them to their present home in Wisconsin. Astor died in 1848, at the age of eighty-five, by then the richest man in America.

JAMES FENIMORE COOPER died in 1851, at the age of sixty-two.

FRANCIS BANNERMAN, one of the world's most successful surplus arms merchants, died in 1918.

All African-American male descendants of the members of the 1st Rhode Island Regiment today are eligible for membership in the Sons of the Revolution, just as female descendants are entitled to membership in the Daughters of the American Revolution.

# Bibliographic Note

*PRIMARY SOURCE MATERIALS* on which this book is based are credited in the text or footnoted. Special acknowledgement is due to four invaluable reference works: Peter Force's monumental multivolume collection of Revolutionary era documents, assembled and published as Force's *American Archives* in Washington, D.C., from 1837 to 1853; Howard H. Peckham's *The Toll of Independence* and Mark Mayo Boatner III's *Encyclopedia of the American Revolution*, both published in 1974; and Robert W. Coakley and Stetson Conn's *War of the American Revolution*, published in 1975 by the United States Army's Center of Military History. Each of these works made preparation of this book a lot easier.

# Index

## L'ENVOI
### (with a nod to Dr. Johnson)

"Depend upon it, Sir: When a man knows he is to be blind in a fortnight, it concentrates his reading wonderfully."